Stories of Strength, Kindness, and the Impact of Women Supporting Each Other

she wins

NICE GIRLS FINISH FIRST

HANNA OLIVAS
Along with 35 Inspiring Authors

TABLE OF CONTENTS

INTRODUCTION

She Wins: Nice Girls Finish First is more than a book—it is a declaration. A declaration that kindness is not a weakness, but a force. That compassion can be a strategy. That resilience wrapped in grace is one of the most powerful tools a woman can possess.

In these pages, you will meet women who have dared to defy the outdated notion that success requires ruthlessness. They come from different backgrounds, cultures, and life experiences, but they all share a common thread: they chose to lead with heart. And in doing so, they didn't just survive their challenges—they conquered them.

Each story in this collection is a testament to the quiet power of empathy, the strength in authenticity, and the courage it takes to remain true to oneself in a world that often rewards the opposite. These women didn't compromise their values to win. Instead, they redefined what it means to win.

Whether you are standing at the edge of a new beginning or picking yourself up from a setback, this book offers more than inspiration— it offers proof. Proof that "nice" girls not only finish—but finish first.

Welcome to a celebration of strength in softness, victory in vulnerability, and power in being unapologetically kind. Welcome to *She Wins*.

Hanna Olivas

Founder and CEO of SHE RISES STUDIOS

https://www.linkedin.com/company/she-rises-studios/
https://www.facebook.com/sherisesstudios
https://www.instagram.com/sherisesstudios_llc/
www.SheRisesStudios.com

Author, Speaker, and Founder. Hanna was born and raised in Las Vegas, Nevada, and has paved her way to becoming one of the most influential women of 2022. Hanna is the co-founder of She Rises Studios and the founder of the Brave & Beautiful Blood Cancer Foundation. Her journey started in 2017 when she was first diagnosed with Multiple Myeloma, an incurable blood cancer. Now more than ever, her focus is to empower other women to become leaders because The Future is Female. She is currently traveling and speaking publicly to women to educate them on entrepreneurship, leadership, and owning the female power within.

She Wins: Nice Girls Finish First in Life and Business

By Hanna Olivas

They didn't see the nights I cried.
Alone.
In silence.
Trying to figure out what I had done to deserve the betrayal.

I had believed in these women. I poured into them, gave them platforms, exposure, community, even friendship. I cheered when they won—even if I was barely surviving. I stood in their corner while they quietly tore me apart behind closed doors.

Some of them smiled in my face.
Hugged me.
Told me they "loved what I was doing."

Then they'd create their own version of my programs. They'd recruit my team behind my back. They'd spread whispers that tried to stain the truth.

And the worst part?

Some days, I still wanted their approval.
That part breaks my heart the most.

I've had to sit with the question:
Why do I crave connection with people who harm me?

I think it's because I've always led with love.
And when you lead with love, the pain cuts deeper.

There was one particular moment, early on, when I had just launched a new project that meant everything to me. A woman I had mentored—and trusted—said behind my back, "She's too emotional to run something this big."

Too emotional.

That phrase haunted me.
I sat in my car that night, hands gripping the steering wheel, sobbing until my body shook.

What she didn't know—what most don't—is that my "too emotional" came from surviving hell and still choosing to show up with a soft heart.

She didn't know I had cried over lost babies.
She didn't know I had begged God to heal me from cancer.
She didn't know what it took to fight for my marriage.
She didn't know I raised five kids while building empires.
She didn't know I was navigating autoimmune flare-ups while smiling on stage.

She saw emotion and mistook it for weakness.
But my tears were not weakness.
They were war cries.

I've been bullied.
And not by trolls or strangers.
By women who once called me "sister."

They formed circles I wasn't invited to.
They used their platforms to hint, jab, throw shade.
They said things like, "Well, Hanna's just a brand. She's not real."

Let me be crystal clear.

I am a mother.
A grandmother.
A CEO.
A wife.
A warrior.

And if being all of that and still standing makes me "just a brand,"
Then honey—brand me.

But I want to be honest with you.

It almost broke me.

There was a time when I shut down.

I stopped showing up online.
I canceled calls.
I let opportunities slide.

I isolated. I questioned God.
"Why would you give me this vision and let it hurt so much to carry?"

And you know what I heard back?

Because you're the one who will make it safe for other women to rise.

That moment changed me.
Not in a big, dramatic fireworks kind of way.
But in the quiet.

I got back up.

Not with fire.
But with faith.

And that's when She Wins Women's Network was born.

Not out of strategy.
But survival.
Not out of ego.
But empathy.

I wanted to create something no woman could ever be excluded from.
A network where your success was celebrated, not silenced.
A table where we pass the mic, not pull it away.

A sisterhood that's real. Raw. Built on healing and honesty.

This book? This chapter? This movement?
It's not for the ones who play nice to your face and vicious behind your back.

It's for the ones who've felt that sting and chose to heal instead of hate.

Let me tell you what happens when a nice girl decides to no longer apologize for being powerful.

She becomes unshakable.

She creates businesses that change lives.
She uses her voice—not to fit in, but to free others.
She stops making herself small to keep the peace.
She builds her own damn table and invites everyone with pure intentions to sit beside her.

I know this because I lived it.

And yes, I'm still nice.
But I'm also a storm wrapped in softness.
And I will no longer carry guilt for that.

The women in this book have stories like mine.
They've been burned.
They've been shut out.
They've had dreams dismissed, voices quieted, talents underestimated.

But we're not here to shame the past.

We're here to rebuild what was broken.

We're here to show the world that you can be kind and still win.

That you can lead with compassion and still command a room.

That you can love deeply and still protect your peace.
That you can celebrate others without sacrificing your own worth.

We are flipping the script.
We are taking back the phrase "nice girls finish last" and writing a new ending.

Nice girls finish first—because we're done finishing behind people who never clapped for us.

We finish first—because we do the work.
We show up.
We feel deeply.
We lead with our whole hearts.
We get back up—again and again.

I created this book because I was done being quiet about the pain.
I was done pretending it didn't happen.
I was done letting the fear of being "too much" or "too emotional" keep me from telling the truth.

Because someone out there is reading this right now thinking, "Maybe it's just me."

It's not.
And it never was.

You're not alone.
And you're not crazy.
You've just been swimming in a system that rewards power plays over purpose.

But not here.
Not with us.

Let me leave you with this—

If you've ever been told you're "too much" or "too soft" or "not enough"...

If you've ever been left out, talked about, or betrayed by the very women you trusted most...

If you've ever questioned your calling because the path got so heavy you couldn't breathe...

I see you.
I am you.

And I built this entire world so you'd have a place to land.

We are done playing small to make insecure people feel comfortable.
We are done pretending we're okay just to keep the peace.
We are done waiting for permission to rise.

You are not too much.
You are not too kind.
You are exactly who this world needs—just as you are.

And if no one else has told you lately, let me:

You win.
You've already won.
Just by surviving.
Just by staying soft in a world that tried to harden you.

Now come win with us.
Join the movement.
Be part of the sisterhood.
Let's change the narrative for women in life and business—together.

Join us at www.shewinswomensnetwork.com

Heather Hanson

Flourish Nutritional Therapy Consultant
Gut-Brain Synergy Coach

https://www.linkedin.com/in/heather-hanson-870752b1/
https://www.facebook.com/flourishntp
https://www.instagram.com/flourishnutritionaltherapy/
https://flourishnutritionaltherapy.com

Heather Hanson, known as the Gut Health Paramedic, is a best-selling author, speaker, and wellness expert specializing in digestive health and mindset transformation. With over 26 years in healthcare, she helps women struggling with bloating, fatigue, and brain fog reclaim their vitality through her Digestive CPR and Mindset Revive frameworks. Her mission is deeply personal—after overcoming autoimmune thyroid disease using her own methodologies, Heather understands the frustration of feeling unheard by conventional medicine. This fueled her passion to uncover the root causes of chronic symptoms, combining digestive health, hormone balance, detoxification, and mindset shifts to help others heal at a cellular level. Through speaking, writing, and coaching, Heather empowers individuals to see symptoms as signals, not setbacks. She provides clear, actionable roadmaps for healing, guiding clients to break free from cycles of pain and limitation. Her work instills hope, connection, and a plan—helping others thrive, not just survive.

She Wins: The Strength in Kindness

By Heather Hanson

For years, I believed that survival meant toughness—that I had to armor myself against the world to prove my worth. Life had taught me that kindness could be mistaken for weakness and that vulnerability was a liability. But through my journey of overcoming deep-rooted trauma, self-doubt, and the battle within my own body, I discovered that true strength lies not in shutting the world out, but in showing up with compassion, resilience, and unwavering self-belief.

The Battle Within

As a child, I learned to read between the lines of people's words, to anticipate danger, and to silence my own needs. My home was not a safe haven; it was a battlefield where I was expected to shrink, endure, and survive. I carried the weight of that fear into adulthood, believing that control—of my body, my emotions, my circumstances—was the only way to keep myself safe.

My body became the reflection of my inner war. Bloating, fatigue, brain fog, and unexplained symptoms became my daily reality, but I ignored them. Instead of listening to the messages my body was sending, I punished it through restriction, over-exercising, and an endless pursuit of an unattainable perfection. I believed that if I could just be *enough*—thin enough, successful enough, pleasing enough—then I would finally feel worthy.

But the truth was, my suffering wasn't coming from my circumstances. It was coming from the beliefs I held about myself. The belief that I had to prove my worth. The belief that kindness meant being taken advantage of. The belief that strength required hardness, rather than grace. These thoughts weren't just affecting my mind—they were manifesting in my body, creating a cycle of stress, illness, and exhaustion that no diet or doctor could fix.

The Shift: Choosing Kindness for Myself

The moment everything changed wasn't dramatic. There was no grand revelation, no overnight transformation. It happened in a quiet realization—an understanding that the very things I had been running from were the keys to my freedom. My body wasn't betraying me; it was begging me to listen. And the strength I had been seeking? It wasn't in perfection. It was in learning to be kind to myself.

Kindness started as a whisper. It was in the small decisions— choosing to rest instead of pushing through exhaustion, nourishing instead of punishing, allowing myself to take up space instead of shrinking. It was in the courage to set boundaries, to say no without guilt, to trust that I was worthy—not because of what I did, but because of who I was.

As I softened toward myself, something incredible happened. The symptoms that had plagued me for years began to ease. My energy returned. My body, once trapped in a cycle of stress and depletion, started to heal. And for the first time, I saw kindness not as a weakness, but as the most powerful force I had ever known.

The Journey to Finding My Passion and Creating Success

On March 20, 2019, I made one of the hardest and most pivotal decisions of my life: I resigned from a practice I had poured my heart, soul, and countless hours into building. It wasn't just a job—it was my baby. Walking away felt like stepping off a cliff, but it was clear that the environment, riddled with lies, broken promises, and toxicity, no longer aligned with my vision or values.

The decision was agonizing, compounded by a deep personal betrayal. A friend I had trusted like family, someone I thought shared my dreams, had revealed his true character. My husband had warned me, but I chose to see the good in people. That optimism had served me well in life, but this time it brought heartache. Still, I knew deep down it was time to break free and follow my passion.

But before I reached that moment of clarity, I went through a period of intense anger, physical and mental exhaustion, and outrage. I spent years operating in survival mode, pushing my body beyond its limits, believing that sheer willpower could override the signals of burnout. The weight of betrayal, stress, and overwork had drained me, but I refused to acknowledge it—until my body gave me no choice.

I remember the exact moment I finally understood what adrenal burnout was. I was in the middle of a workout, doing what I had always done—pushing myself hard, ignoring the warning signs. And then, for the first time in my life, I had to stop. My body simply wouldn't go any further. My heart was pounding, my limbs felt like lead, and an overwhelming wave of exhaustion crashed over me. I sat down, stunned and defeated. I had always been the person who could push through anything, but now, my body was saying, "No more."

That moment forced me to confront the truth—I was completely depleted. My nervous system had been in overdrive for so long that it had nothing left to give. The rage, the stress, the relentless pursuit of proving my worth had taken its toll. I had ignored the signs of burnout until they became impossible to dismiss. I resigned that very day.

Within 72 hours of resigning, I had formed my LLC, reclaiming a name I'd once casually used for a hobby nutrition practice. It was as if the universe had been waiting for me to take this leap. At that moment, I became unstoppable. Nothing—and no one—was going to stand in my way.

As I reflect on my journey, I see how every job, every challenge, and every heartbreak prepared me for this path. The years I spent building others' practices taught me invaluable lessons about leadership, resilience, and the art of transformation. Each experience shaped me into the person I am today—a woman determined to create a safe, empowering space for others to heal and thrive.

The Power of Kindness in Leadership and Success

The world often tells women that in order to succeed, we must be ruthless—that we must suppress our emotions, toughen up, and play by the rules of competition. But I have found the opposite to be true.

True leadership—whether in business, relationships, or personal growth—comes from **compassion, connection, and authenticity**. When we lead with kindness, we build trust. When we uplift others instead of tearing them down, we create communities where success is shared. And when we embrace our full selves—strengths, flaws, and all—we inspire others to do the same.

Kindness is not passive. It is not about being a pushover or letting people take advantage of us. It is about having the strength to be vulnerable, the courage to stand in our truth, and the resilience to keep going even when life tries to break us. Kindness is setting boundaries. Kindness is knowing your worth. Kindness is choosing growth over fear.

She Wins

I have walked through fire and emerged not hardened, but softened. Not weaker, but stronger. And I am not alone. Women everywhere are rewriting the narrative—proving that being kind, compassionate, and true to oneself is not just a path to survival, but a path to success.

We are not winning *despite* being kind. We are winning *because* of it.

So, to the women who have been told they are too soft, too emotional, too nice—know this: Your kindness is your superpower. Your ability to uplift, connect, and lead with love is what makes you unstoppable. **She wins. You win. We all win—together.**

Let's Connect

If my journey resonates with you, and you're ready to step into your power, I'd love to connect. Whether you're looking to break free from limiting beliefs, reclaim your health, or build a life that aligns with your deepest desires, I am here to guide you. Let's take this journey together—because you are capable of more than you ever imagined. Reach out to me today, and let's start creating the future you deserve.

Hunyah Irfan

HunyahTravels
Content Creator

https://ca.linkedin.com/in/hunyah-irfan-blogger351
https://www.facebook.com/OfficialHunyahTravels
https://www.instagram.com/officalhunyahtravels
https://www.youtube.com/@officalhunyahtravels1

Hunyah is a 32-year-old content creator with a community development background. Hunyah currently facilates at Western University for spoken word and poetry in disabled arts .Hunyah has picked a lot in the journey of being a content creator. Hunyah will share her experience when getting pick up on towards career.

Internally Being Bullied

By Hunyah Irfan

Hi,

My name is Hunyah Irfan. As you know, I'm a content creator and I do a lot of things in the community.

Being successful is great.

But no one sees that being internally bullied is something that I deal with.

That is because bullying is caused by relatives in my family through my dad's side.

Here are a few things you should know.

1. While growing up, I got picked on by a lot because people thought I wasn't smart
2. There was a rumor in school because I liked a kid in the class that went on a little bit until high school
3. Being bullied by my relatives is something hard to deal with

What is the reason?

Internally bullied is being picked on at home because of your knowledge.

For me, that is because my dad's side cousin also has a YouTube channel, but they are monetized. Also, their content is only against people.

I have been doing content creation for about six years now. My content creation is about food and travel, and what I do.

It is not against people.

Factors to know

1. Gender stereotypes
2. Competing with women because of the YouTube channel
3. Greed from my cousins who have with YouTube
4. Hard earning

The reason why there are gender stereotypes is that my cousin from my dad's side competes with me because I'm a woman.

And he is a man. That can lead to serious problems.

As of right now, there are many places that say a man should be competing against a woman.

Another thing, my dad's side cousins are greedy.

That is because right now I have 164 subscribers, and my dad's side cousin has 1 million subscribers. That cousin wants to take my 164 subscribers when he has 1 million subscribers already.

My dad's side cousins think that only they are the people who can have a YouTube channel.

That no one else can.

That is where the problem is coming from.

On top of that, my aunts and uncles from my dad's side don't take my side, they only go for those cousins.

That is why there is a lot of internal bullying I face.

Education is key

The difference between me and my dad's side cousins is education.

I might have fewer subscribers, but I have a good presence on social media.

I facilitate and I'm very involved in the community, but I'm also educated.

My dad's side cousins have a lot of subscribers, but they are not so educated.

That is not because of being overseas, that is because overall.

I use my education in a good way.

My dad's side cousins don't give any importance to their education.

It is only what they want to do.

What are the main reasons why my dad's side cousins don't get along?

The main reason is the jealousy that my dad's side cousin has.

I was brought up in Canada, yet my dad's side cousins have no exposure to any other country except for back home.

Also, they never liked me growing up because of my English, and I knew a lot more about traveling than they did.

If you are being internally bullied, what should you do?

1. Talk to a friend or another relative
2. Speak to a therapist
3. Block people when needed
4. Don't listen to negative stuff
5. Move on

Can you sometimes tell if you are being bullied or not?

From my experience, I can tell that I'm being bullied. But not everyone is ready to listen. My dad's side never listened to my view on being compared with my cousin's YouTube channel back home.

Then, in social groups dealing with a jealous content creator in the community. That is another problem.

Having a former employer spreading rumors and sending indirect messages is also bullying.

For example, my story about being bullied couldn't be shared until now.

On how much I have been bullied because I have a skill or some success that the other person is different.

When I wanted to get married to the guy I liked in my early 20s, I got bullied on that too really badly. That is because the guy was from my mom's side. That itself is a long story.

Then, my former employer didn't accept the way I offered something better. The rumors she spread about me were shocking, that I wasn't recognized for my work, even because I had a skill or something that the other person didn't know.

This is what happens when you are internally bullied.

This is my story of being bullied. I hope you enjoyed reading my story of how I faced bullying.

Susan M Tatem

Founder and CEO of Bright Path Coaching
Coach & Author

https://www.facebook.com/SusanMTatem
https://brightpath4autism.org

Susan Tatem, the founder of Bright Path Coaching, is dedicated to empowering families of children with autism 12 years and older to navigate school and the transition into independent adulthood. Inspired by her own journey as a single mom raising a daughter with autism, Susan combines personal experience, professional expertise from 30 years in healthcare, and a deep passion to guide families with compassion and clarity. Her coaching provides parents with the tools to create a clear path for their children's future, addressing challenges like workforce readiness, independent living, and social skills. Susan's ultimate vision is to establish supported living communities worldwide, where young adults with autism can thrive. With honesty, integrity, and a heart for service, Bright Path Coaching equips families to transform worry into confidence, ensuring every individual with autism has the opportunity to lead a fulfilled, independent life. Additionally, Susan is the Managing Partner of the Tidewater Virginia Chapter of the She Wins Women's Network. She

Wins is all about empowering women entrepreneurs and professionals to connect, collaborate, and grow. It's a space where we can build meaningful relationships, elevate our businesses, and truly thrive shoulder to shoulder. Let's rise and win together!

My Autism Mom Transformation Journey

By Susan M Tatem

The term "nice girls" often carries an undertone of underestimation, as though kindness and compassion are weaknesses in a world that values boldness and ambition. My journey proves otherwise. Nice girls, when fueled by resilience, faith, and purpose, not only finish but finish first—transforming lives along the way.

A Mother's Journey

My story began with an unshakable love for my daughter, a love that would be tested and refined as we faced life's challenges together. When my daughter was about three years old, I began to notice differences in her. She no longer seemed to be developing along the normal benchmarks for her age, nor keeping up with her peers. I knew something was wrong. I had her tested, and she was diagnosed with developmental delay.

"Take a deep breath," I thought, "Let it wash over you. It's not the end of the world. She can catch up with some help."

I put her in Head Start Preschool, which was a special program for those kids who were a little behind and needed some extra support. I was convinced that this would do the trick and she would be fine. After all, I had been a distinguished honor student, member of the National Honor Society, and Presidential Academic Fitness Award recipient. Surely, my daughter would be as well.

As time went on, it became clear that would not be the case. In second grade, she would hide under her desk, crying for almost the entire day. She was struggling with her coursework, especially math. At her triennial IEP meeting that spring, I practically begged them to repeat second grade. Not only did they refuse, but they locked us in the room and badgered us until we signed consent to discontinue her IEP plan altogether. I was utterly stunned, crushed, and heartbroken. I felt so betrayed because I had trusted that they would have my daughter's best interests at heart. Nothing could have been farther from the truth.

In third grade, the school has a meeting with all the parents to go over the SOL testing their child is required to pass, which includes multiplication and division. My daughter could not even do addition. At her next meeting, I expressed that there was absolutely no way my daughter could pass the SOLs, and she is being set up for failure. The general consensus was that they didn't care. I was so discouraged I didn't know what to do.

By the hand of providence, I was invited by a coworker to a weekend craft retreat. There I met a group of women that would change our lives forever. Several ladies worked in a neighboring school system and strongly encouraged me to homeschool my daughter. I thought this would

be impossible because I was a single mom, but they laid out how it would work. This was a complete game-changer!

"Even if I am absolutely terrible at homeschooling," I thought, "I can't possibly do any worse than they are doing!"

I picked my daughter up from school for Christmas break and told them she would not be back. It was not an easy task, but in six months, I had increased my daughter's math skills by an entire grade level! I was elated. I found the answer... or so I thought.

When my daughter was diagnosed with autism at age 10, the world suddenly felt heavier. I didn't know anything about autism. I was a single mom with limited resources and a thousand questions. How would I support her? How would I guide her into a life filled with opportunity and independence? All my dreams for her seemed crushed. What do I do now? I knew one thing for certain: I was never going to let anyone steamroll over her like the school system had ever again!

In those early days, being "nice" didn't mean avoiding the fight or folding; it meant stepping into the ring with determination wrapped in kindness. I became her fiercest advocate, learning everything I could about autism, therapies, and educational options. Along the way, I encountered many obstacles—bureaucracy, misunderstanding, and exhaustion—but I also met people whose kindness and knowledge inspired me. Chief among them was an advocate, Rachel, who would forever change the course of our lives.

This advocate, with her patience and wisdom, taught me how to navigate the complexities of raising a child with autism. She showed me that kindness paired with tenacity and persistence could open doors that seemed sealed shut. When Rachel passed away, her loss was profound, but so was her impact. I vowed to honor her legacy by becoming that same source of support and guidance for other families.

Kindness as Strength

Being nice isn't about pleasing everyone or avoiding conflict; it's about approaching challenges with grace, empathy, and a deep-seated belief that good can prevail. As a single mom, I wore many hats: provider, physical therapist assistant, advocate, teacher, and homeschool educator. Each role demanded a delicate balance of compassion and strength.

Homeschooling my daughter while managing a full-time career was a daily lesson in patience and perseverance. Every milestone she achieved was a testament to our hard work, and every setback was an opportunity to learn. I wasn't just teaching her academic lessons; I was teaching her life skills, resilience, and the importance of kindness.

Finding My Calling

As my daughter grew older, new challenges emerged. The question that haunted me—and many other parents in the autism community—was this: What happens after high school? The support systems that guided us through her younger years were disappearing, and the transition to adulthood loomed large. I realized that many parents were just as overwhelmed as I was, unsure of how to help their children navigate this uncharted territory.

Around the same time, my health began to decline. Chronic pain and physical limitations forced me to reevaluate my future. I could have let these challenges defeat me, but instead, they became the catalyst for something greater. It was during this period of reflection that I discovered my true calling: to create a path for young adults with autism to transition into independent, fulfilling lives—and to guide their families with the kindness and determination that had carried me through my own journey.

Building Bright Path Coaching

Starting Bright Path Coaching wasn't easy. I was stepping into unfamiliar territory, learning about sales, business development, and the many moving parts of entrepreneurship. But I was driven by a mission bigger than myself.

At its core, Bright Path Coaching is about empowerment. I guide parents from feelings of overwhelm and fear to confidence and clarity. My five-stage process provides families with actionable steps to help their children gain life skills, build independence, and thrive as adults. I've learned that kindness, paired with a structured plan, can move mountains.

My clients walk away with a 90-day action plan based on the three pillars of long-term success for their kids with autism: Research, Advocate, Facilitate.

The Power of Faith

My faith has been the cornerstone of every decision I've made. I believe that God placed this mission in my heart, and I've leaned on Him during moments of doubt and struggle. Faith doesn't make the path easy, but it does make the journey purposeful.

When I started this business, I often wondered if being "nice" was enough in a competitive world. But I realized that my authenticity, compassion, and unwavering belief in the potential of every individual with autism were my greatest strengths. Parents don't come to me for flash or gimmicks; they come to me because they know I care deeply about their children and their futures.

From Vision to Reality

The vision for Bright Path Coaching extends far beyond one-on-one coaching. I'm researching the founding of supported living communities where young adults with autism can develop life skills for independence with the help of neurotypical mentors. I'm working on writing books, speaking on stages, and offering online programs to expand my reach and impact.

Nice Girls Do Finish First

This journey has taught me that kindness isn't a weakness—it's a superpower. It's the ability to connect with others on a deeper level, to inspire trust, and to make meaningful change. Being nice doesn't mean avoiding challenges; it means tackling them with empathy and grace.

I've faced challenges that could have broken me—health struggles, single parenthood, and the daunting task of starting a business from scratch. But I've risen above them, fueled by faith, determination, and a heart committed to serving others.

Today, as the founder of Bright Path Coaching, I'm proud to say that nice girls do finish first. We finish with integrity, with purpose, and with the profound knowledge that our kindness has the power to change lives.

Nice girls don't just finish; they change the world along the way.

Hannah Darby GMBPsP SMACCPH

Healing with Hannah
Therapist: Founder of Kintsugi Method with H.E.A.L approach

https://www.linkedin.com/in/hannahdarbyhealingwithhannah
https://www.facebook.com/hannahsdarby
https://www.instagram.com/healingwithhannahd/
https://www.healingwithhannah.co.uk
https://www.accph.org.uk/united-kingdom/martley/therapists-and-coaches/hannah-darby

Hannah Darby GMBPsP SMACCPH is an award winning trauma therapist who helps guide individuals on their personal grief journey. Hannah's unique Kintsgui Method and H.E.A.L approach has been featured in the international magazines, She Wins and Becoming an Unstoppable Woman. Hannah is a General Member of the British Psychological Society, a Senior Member of Accredited Counsellors, Coaches, Psychotherapists and Hypnotherapists, a Reiki Master, a HeartHealing® practitioner, Masseuse and an International Bestselling Author. Hannah runs Healing with Hannah, a unique therapy practice based on her professional and personal wisdom guided by science and spirituality. Hannah guides people on their personal grief journeys with care and compassion.

Hannah works with their mind, heart and body to help them find deep healing with soulful integration. Hannah resides in the British Countryside with her husband, four cats and two chihuahuas. Hannah loves heavy metal, horror movies and long country walks.

Ignite your Inner Power with Kindness

By Hannah Darby GMBPsP SMACCPH

The saying goes 'Nice girls finish last,' but I beg to differ. So should you! It is through our kindness that our true colours shine the brightest. Through our kindness, we grow and create opportunities for ourselves. With care and compassion, we can unite and build a better future. After all, it takes far fewer muscles to smile than it does to frown!

Rising up against the hate in the world takes far more courage, more strength and more resilience than sinking down to their level. Kindness is a strength, never a weakness. I'm here to show you that nice girls do finish first.

Growing up was tough for me. I was severely bullied, I had chronic health issues and I experienced parental death at only 13. In fact, I was bullied all the way through my education and later in the workplace, too. Why? Because I was nice! I was a quiet kid, I was small, I was timid, I was different, I was nice. This made me an easy target for the bullies. I pride myself on the fact that I never sank down to their level. I stayed nice. But being nice doesn't mean that you are a pushover. It doesn't mean you can't hold healthy boundaries. It doesn't mean you can't become a strong independent woman that the world will think twice about messing with.

It took me great strength and courage to rise against this negativity in my life. I have always prided myself on my compassionate and kind nature. I was not going to let the bullies take it away from me. I am proud that I never reacted to their comments. I would not feed into the narrative they were trying to write about me. I refused for them to kill my kindness. I stood strong in my belief that nice girls can and do finish first.

The other girls in the school, college, university and later in multiple workplaces would talk quietly about me behind my back, pointing, laughing, generally being complete bitches! For a long time, I used to pretend I couldn't hear their comments. They were all different yet essentially the same, lost in their own pain. They were deflecting their own insecurities onto the easiest target, me. Why? Because they did not have the emotional intelligence or the emotional maturity to cope with their issues. I, on the other hand, did not use my father's death to turn myself into one of those hate spreaders. Even though I was full of anger, I continued to stay true to my nature and uphold my kindness to others.

I have always been alternative, never a classic girly girl. I hated pink dresses. In fact, I hated anything overly girly, and most of my friends were guys. When I was 17, I got dreadlocks that I still proudly have today over 20 years later. I was different. I stood out. This made me an easy target. However, I pride myself on my differences. On my uniqueness, as this is what makes me, me. It's where my inner power lies. I will never dim my light for anyone.

Let me take you back to one of the most profound bullying experiences I have been unfortunate enough to go through. I live in the British countryside and had a long-hour bus ride into the city to our local sixth form college. I dreaded getting on that bus. The thought of it brought on panic attacks, sweaty palms and negative intrusive thoughts. All these years later, it still makes me feel a bit funny now when I think about it.

Every single day there was a group of four girls who would pick on me, bitch about me, comment on my clothes, my hair, my makeup, generally picking apart every thing about me. Making me feel inadequate, making me feel like a freak. The worst thing was they wouldn't do it if they thought I could hear them. This made me feel crazy. I had a portable CD player I used to listen to on the journey to college. Every day, as soon as I put my headphones in, they would start their narrative of hate against me. Picking on my giant flares, my dark makeup, my choice of Metal music, even the way I sat down on the chair! They didn't realise that a lot of the time I put my headphones in, but didn't press play. I could hear everything they said about me. Making me feel paranoid, everyone was out to get me. It destroyed my trust in others and started to infect my inner mind with negativity. This took me a long time to get over, a long time to be able to trust other people again, especially women.

I am proud, I never showed them how much they hurt me. I never changed the way I dressed, the way I walked, the way I sat, or changed how I did my makeup. I didn't want to give them the pleasure of knowing that they had hurt me, upset me. Deep down on the inside, though, it caused me so much hurt and pain. I took this pain out on myself, with self-harm, drugs and alcohol. Their words cut me deeply, due to my caring, empathic nature. I absorbed it all, every single word.

After hearing so many negative comments in my outside world, eventually, they filtered into my inside world too. I started to talk negatively to myself, believing the hurtful things that they used to say. They built on the fear and doubt that had been seeded when my father died in front of me. Words are far mightier than the sword and can cause so much more damage to our self-esteem than a punch in the face. Sometimes, I wish they had just punched me instead. Like that would have affected me less, would have caused less lasting damage. Once those negative seeds have been sown, they grow thick and fast in our mind, choking the beautiful garden that had been growing before.

If I could go back and speak to the younger me, I would give her a massive hug. She had the courage to stay true to her beliefs and never changed herself to fit in. I would show her how amazing she is. Show her everything we are going to achieve and give her the confidence boost that teenage me so desperately needed. I always thought of a witty response hours after it had occurred, but at the time, I was frozen in fear.

I realise now, they were just jealous of me. Jealous of my beauty on the inside and the outside. Jealous of my strength and intelligence. Jealous that most of my friends were guys. Jealous of the nice girl that I am. They were deflecting their own pain and hurt, from their own trauma onto me, as I was an easy target. They did not have any other outlet for their pain, so they used me to feel better about themselves.

Now, I hold my head high with confidence. I never let them break me down permanently. I have rewritten the narrative in my mind to one of positivity, love and compassion for myself. I have reconnected to my inner power that grows from my compassionate, empathic nature. I am a nice girl who finished first. I never changed who I was, I stayed true to myself. This takes far more strength, courage and resilience than being nasty ever does.

I may have missed some college classes because of them, but I still achieved good grades. I may have fallen into addiction, but I eventually pulled myself out. I may have self-harmed as a way to gain control back. They even drew me so low, along with the grief from the death of my father, that I contemplated suicide, but I am still here today. I have become a beacon of strength and inspiration for others. This is something I am truly proud of. I continued my nice girl traits and studied Psychology and Criminology at university because I wanted to help others. I have always known I was here to listen in a non-judgemental way, to hold a space for and support those in need.

Kindness is a strength, not a weakness. I now run an award-winning therapy business—Healing with Hannah. I am a guiding light for others who have experienced loss and grief. I turned my kindness into my profession. I found that the strength in kindness is far stronger than that in nastiness. I know now that these experiences I went through are a testimony to my strength, my courage, my resilience, my inner power. I am so grateful that I get to share my journey with you. So you may find the strength and resilience to stay nice, knowing that you too can be a woman who wins.

Remember, nice girls DO and will always finish first.

Tammy Cameron

Calm Strategy
Holistic Educator

https://www.facebook.com/Calm.Strategy
https://www.instagram.com/tammystma/
https://calmstrategy.ca/

Tammy is a compassionate educator with a passion for reading, writing, and all forms of sharing stories. The stories she writes are stories of courage and connection that engage the reader with new perspectives and a process of inner reflection. Tammy draws on over 25 years of experience in facilitated classroom, boardroom, and conference room adult education and staff training. She has taught at colleges and universities across North America. She delivers practical strategies for developing calm spaces were productivity and creativity shine. Having faced significant health challenges at a young age, she knows struggle and resilience. She has cried intensely over a dropped grape, focused profoundly on breathing to get through extreme physical pain, and has climbed a mountain in high-heeled sandals because she could! She most often writes in the early morning, alongside the sunrise, with a view of pine trees and basswood dancing in a gentle breeze.

Victory Through Voices of Kindness and Grace

By Tammy Cameron

Bullying and its insidious roots take many forms and permeate our world in ways that are indescribable at times. It is an underlying ripple that needs to change, and now is the time. We are all faced with the decision to engage in this web of destruction or to stand powerfully in our own authenticity and emerge in our own light. I will share some small examples here because small does not mean insignificant; your learning and your light, whatever your experience, are brilliantly powerful.

I grew up with an adventurous brother, and some of our daily fun was not what my parents had in mind. Discipline in our family was time alone in our private bedrooms. We were always instructed to "think" about what we had done or not done in these moments of banishment. This led to self-reflection for me on my behavior, decisions, and my core being. I thought about right versus wrong, questioned my own actions and reactions, and examined the environment around me and how I was responding within it. This time taught me deep reflection, a skill that remains and serves me well today.

I encourage anyone experiencing any form of bullying to take a moment and deeply reflect. What do you know to be true? This is where your power lies. When you find, recognize, and honour your truth, you will be powerful beyond measure and no force will bring you down.

I had a childhood bully as early as my kindergarten days. This was a child who was older, bigger, stronger, verbally and sometimes physically aggressive, and who threatened to throw me into the river daily on my way to school. I cried. I pretended to be sick, hoping to stay home. Sometimes, I would leave for school, get a block away from home, see this child waiting for me on the bridge blocking my path, and turn back, not wanting to die that day in the river; this was a real fear as I had been educated about the dangers of cold and deep water. Some days, I crossed to the other side of the street, where there was no sidewalk, to avoid this bully. I tried changing my schedule, leaving earlier or later. Inevitably, many days, I faced this bully, and I had to gather the courage to protect myself somehow with intelligence: words, timing of movement, or avoidance. When these strategies failed, I was left with using my backpack or umbrella as a shield or gripping the bridge railing as strongly as I could to hold my ground. You might wonder where the adults were in this scenario. Well, my parents were there encouraging me, guiding me, and supporting me, but they could not trail me to school every single day; they offered strategies to manage instead. From this experience, I learned to use my voice to speak up about truth, kindness, fairness, and treating others well; this took enormous effort from a shy girl.

Daily, we cross paths with many people, and we have an opportunity to change the world. Fast forward to my adult years, and one morning on my way to an appointment, a woman approached as I was standing at a busy downtown intersection, waiting to cross the street at a red light. She also wanted to cross and quickly made her decision to dart into multiple lanes of oncoming traffic. In the next instant, realizing that she would lose the battle with traffic, she darted back, defeated, and stood beside me impatiently. I turned to her and said, "Your family needs you here." She said, "I'm very late." I repeated, "Your family needs you here." I saw her begin to think about and process my words before she replied, "Thank you. You are right. Thank you." She said this many times. Our conversation was complete. The light turned green, we both crossed, she went her way, and I went mine. This is what deep reflection and practice at using my voice have taught me to do: speak up when you know the message that someone needs to hear and when you can add value to someone's life, even in a seemingly small way. This is just one example of many, because yes, I talk to random strangers when something important needs to be said.

Without awareness, we cannot act. Look around and ask yourself where you can make a positive difference, even if it is a momentary conversation with a stranger. If you have helpful words, say the words with kindness and grace. The words may or may not be received well in sensitive situations, which is true. There is an element of risk involved, and it is worth it because with care and effort, we all win.

Around age thirteen, I had a silent bully. Our shared classroom coat closet at school was like an oversized walk-in closet with two open doorways. Each student had a "tote box," which was a sliding plastic bin on a shelf, and this was the place to store our personal items. The space was not locked or secured in any way. One day, my math textbook went missing. I could not find it and finally reported it to the teacher. Time passed, and my parents became involved, followed by the school principal. Our books were loaned to us for the year by the school, and there were "no more" books available, so I was left to study math, a difficult subject for me, with no book. Worse than this, several weeks later, my textbook reappeared in my tote box, defaced, with scribbles all over many pages; this was black marker, heavy and intentional. I showed the teacher, and I showed my parents. From here, the school accused me of damaging their property and wanted my parents to pay the cost of this textbook because I had "not taken care" of it. My parents argued for consideration of the handwriting. I am left-handed, and I had the artistic writing style of a teenage girl; the marks in this book were careless and determined to have been done by a right-handed person. Thus, the accusation against me was withdrawn, and my parents did not pay. I remained confused about this targeted attack. I never identified the bully. I did learn math. Being accused and blamed for this destruction of property was difficult; however, this experience helped me once again to use my voice and to speak up, this time, with authority figures who are not always right.

Years later, in a classroom where I was the teacher, not the student, I had a young woman in the class who thrived for a while and then stopped attending without explanation. After many weeks, she returned, seeking familiarity; she was sixteen and pregnant. She was not married. Her parents had shunned her. Not wanting shame upon the family, they had banished her from the family home and into a guest house to live alone. She had trouble walking the stairs. She was lonely and scared. She had no job or source of income. She had a friend who would bring her a potato or a tomato here and there, foods that could be taken from a family pantry without notice. I know all of this simply because I began a conversation. I asked, and she shared her story. I suggested that she sleep on the main floor, avoiding stairs, and that she wear a purse at home with her phone inside so that she could call for help when needed. It takes delicate discernment to know which words to use and when it is important to speak up. Fast forward, following some further months of absence, my student returned to visit, this time with a healthy baby boy! As I began teaching the class, the quiet baby on her lap suddenly started kicking his legs with excitement, waving his arms, and making happy gurgling sounds. My student shared, "He knows your voice." From the womb, the baby recognized care and kindness. This is how we win!

Take your experience and transform it. Let your kindness extend to others and continue no matter the circumstance. Do not be broken by the difficult or unfair moments around you. If someone excludes you, empower yourself by choosing to move on; a more deserving and supportive tribe is waiting for you. Ask for and accept support from others when possible. When you think you have failed, reassess and find the ways in which you have succeeded.

"Thank you for caring about me." These words came to me from a student running after me on the street. After months of trying daily to support her through distress and feeling that I had failed to reach her, she acknowledged my efforts. You may not always know your impact at the time; strive for your interactions to spread positivity in some way, and you will make someone else's world better. Seize your meaningful moments at home, at school, at work, in relationships, and in the community. Develop awareness of what is happening around you. Know your truth and use your voice courageously.

Bullying extends far beyond childhood school days and sadly exists on a much grander scale than the small examples shared here. It grows when it continues unaddressed, and it harms everyone. Our call now is to boldly step away from bystander apathy. Step into your own voice. Speak up with kindness and generosity of spirit. Be the light for yourself and for others. This is how she wins!

Thank you to my amazing students for sharing your vulnerabilities and trust. I have learned from you, and I honour every lesson. Thank you, readers, for diving into this topic with us. May we all strive daily to create kind, inclusive, and healthy environments where we all win!

Thank you to all my personal bullies, known and unknown, for my lessons. I accept those lessons, and I move forward; may you also extend the same grace to others. For my moments of reflection, I am grateful.

Where can you make a positive impact today? You are brilliantly powerful. You were never broken. Your experience is significant. Choose kindness as your gift to yourself.

Sonya McDonald

Founder and CEO of Sonya McDonald LLC
Board Certified Transformational Life Coach, Registered Nurse,
International Best Selling Author, and Speaker

https://www.linkedin.com/in/sonya-mcdonald-rn-bsn-bcc-7786521b9/
https://www.facebook.com/sonya.mcdonald.96/
https://www.instagram.com/sonyamcdonald_/
www.sonyamcdonald.com

Sonya McDonald is a much sought-after expert as a Board-Certified Transformational Life Coach, Author, Speaker, and Registered Nurse with 30 years of experience. She received her Board Certification as a LifeCoach from Robbins Madanes Training Institute, the official coach training school of Tony Robbins. She dedicates her life to empowering women to conquer fear, rise above overwhelm, confidently embracing a life of authenticity and fulfillment. Living with Rheumatoid Arthritis and Fibromyalgia for over 16 years, and anxiety since childhood, Sonya proves that chronic and invisible illness does not define you. When she's not spending time with her two beautiful daughters and husband, or walking her dog, Sonya loves ocean sunsets, swimming, and immersing herself in nature. Let her guide you, igniting your inner light and helping you shine brightly, no matter the challenges you face. To learn more about how Sonya can help you, visit her website at www.sonyamcdonald.com.

The Power of Choosing You First

By Sonya McDonald

I was always the nice girl. The one who smiled, who cared, who listened. The one who went the extra mile to make sure everyone else was okay, even if I wasn't. I thought that was how you won in life. By being good, by being kind, by always putting others first, and for a while, it worked.

I built a career as a nurse, pouring love and compassion into my patients, giving my heart to my work. I excelled in every role I stepped into, whether it was caring for critically ill patients or leading teams as a nurse supervisor. I took pride in my work, ensuring that every patient under my care received the best treatment possible. But the more I gave, the more I noticed something: not everyone valued kindness. Some people saw it as a weakness. Others saw it as a threat.

When I was working as a nurse supervisor, managing the preoperative holding areas and ensuring the entire operating room schedule ran smoothly, I thrived. Doctors and colleagues commended my work, they saw my leadership, my ability to keep things running efficiently, and my dedication to patient care. And then, jealousy showed up. One nurse, in particular, didn't like that I was excelling. She didn't like that I was receiving praise. So, instead of supporting the success of our team, she deliberately reassigned me to an area where my skills would be undervalued, a lesser role that didn't challenge me or allow me to make the impact I was capable of.

That was my moment of clarity. I could stay, I could tolerate being pushed down, let someone else dictate my value, and continue to work in a toxic environment that did not appreciate what I brought to the table. Or, I could rise. I could choose myself first and go somewhere that allowed me to thrive.

And when my daughter was little, that choice became even clearer. I was working tirelessly, but the moment I had to take her to the doctor, I was made to feel like I was failing my job for putting my family first. I was not going to apologize for being a good mother. I refused to let guilt control me. I refused to be bullied into thinking that taking care of my child made me any less of a nurse or professional.

So, I made a change. I left that hospital and became a pediatric school nurse. A position where I could continue to serve, using my nursing skills in a way that aligned with my values. It was the best decision I could have made. Because I learned something powerful. When you choose YOU, when you walk away from places that don't appreciate you, you don't lose. You win.

This wasn't the first time I had to make a choice to walk away. Earlier in my career, I worked at another job where the culture was anything but respectful. I remember seeing colleagues throw things in frustration, speak to others with open disrespect, and create an environment that felt chaotic and toxic. As a young nurse and a young mom, I had a decision to make. Would I allow myself to be treated that way? Would I stay in a place that made me feel small, devalued, and belittled? Absolutely not. I refused to fight for my worth in an environment that didn't support me. I refused to tolerate being spoken to in a demeaning manner. So, I made the choice again. I left and found a workplace where professionalism, respect, and kindness mattered.

Twice, I had to walk away. Not because I wasn't strong, but because I knew my worth. Have you ever felt like you were excelling at something, only to have someone try to dim your light? Have you ever put your family first, only to be made to feel guilty for doing so? That was me. I thought my job as a nurse meant putting myself last. That being a good person meant enduring toxicity, ignoring my own needs, and staying in situations that drained my soul.

But that's not winning. That's survival. Winning is setting boundaries. Winning is choosing your well-being over other people's comfort. Winning is walking away from places that make you shrink. So, I made a change. I didn't leave nursing; I evolved. I found healthier environments to work in, where I could thrive without sacrificing myself. And when my Rheumatoid Arthritis progressed, making clinical nursing more physically challenging, I knew it was time to expand my purpose.

I took my nursing background, my heart for helping others, and my ability to uplift and heal, and I transformed them into a mission. I became a transformational life coach, a speaker, and an author, using my experiences to help even more people, not just in hospitals, but in their personal lives, careers, and health journeys. That's when I truly started winning.

People watched. They saw me shift, not in anger, not in bitterness, but in strength. They saw that you could be kind and still be strong. That you could be compassionate without being a pushover. That you could love deeply without letting toxicity take root. And some? Well, they didn't like it.

There will always be people who want you to match their energy. They want you to snap back, to engage in the drama, to play the game. And when you don't? When you refuse to let their moods dictate yours? They get uncomfortable. But that's not your problem. Because here's the secret. You don't have to play the game to win it. You rise above it. And that's exactly what I did.

People think winning means being the loudest in the room. The toughest. The one who fights back harder, who stands their ground with clenched fists and a sharp tongue. But real winning? It's peace. It's not letting the world harden you. It's having a life that's lighter because you refuse to carry the weight of bitterness and resentment. And when you lift yourself up, you have the strength to lift others.

My journey as a nurse wasn't over. If anything, it had evolved. I was still serving. I was still using my skills. But now, I was doing it in a way that allowed me to thrive through coaching, speaking, and writing, all while continuing to honor my passion for healing. This isn't just my work. It's my mission. And the best part? I still win. Not by playing their game, but by rewriting the rules.

Winning isn't about being the loudest or the toughest. It's about choosing yourself, standing in your truth, and refusing to shrink. It's about walking through life unshaken by fear, untamed by doubt, and unapologetically authentic. That is exactly what I help women do.

As a transformational life coach, my mission is to empower women to ignite their light and transform their lives. I help women conquer fear, rise above overwhelm, and confidently step fully into the authentic life they were meant to live. I guide them to shine so bright that nothing can dim their power. I work with women who are ready to live authentically and fearlessly, to break free from limitations, and to step into a life filled with purpose, peace, and unstoppable energy. Whether you're overcoming self-doubt, battling health challenges, or simply searching for more, know this. You are made for more. You are a winner.

Through my coaching, I help women increase their energy tenfold, double their peace, and step into a stress-free life filled with love and abundance. You deserve to thrive, not just survive. If you're ready to rise, visit **www.sonyamcdonald.com** and take the first step toward your transformation. If you're ready to break free from limitations, this is your time. Ignite your light, transform your life, love yourself fiercely, and step into your power, because when you do, you WIN.

You are not here to play small. You were created for greatness, to step into the highest version of yourself, and to walk with purpose. No matter what has tried to hold you back—fear, doubt, limitations, or the voices of those who didn't believe in you—it's time to break free.

Your journey doesn't end with the challenges you've faced. It begins with how you rise from them.

When I chose to stand in my power, everything changed. I stopped seeking validation from places that could never see my worth. I stopped allowing other people's negativity to define my success. I stopped playing by the rules that were designed to keep me small. Instead, I built a new path, one that honors my purpose, my voice, and my mission.

You don't have to wait for permission. You don't have to wait for the perfect moment. Ignite your light, transform your life, and step boldly into your greatness. Because when you choose yourself first, when you step into your power, you don't just win, you thrive!

Maureen Denise

CEO of Diva Designs Hair Studio

https://www.linkedin.com/in/dr-maureen-mcdonald-watkins-dpc-chw-cha-66b13559/
https://www.facebook.com/nesi.mcdonaldwatkins/
https://www.instagram.com/nesiisflawless/

Maureen McDonald was born January 21, 1967, in South Carolina. With a lifetime of experience as a mother of two and a grandmother of three, a significant challenge in my early years demanded resilience, fueling my determination and discovering talents that would guide my future. My journey eventually led me to beauty and fashion, where my passion flourished. After graduating from beauty school with a focus on hair, I continued my education at the National Institute of Cosmetology, ultimately earning a doctorate in the field. For over 30 years, I owned and operated a salon, using my skills to serve and uplift my community. My love for bringing people together inspired me to host creative events, fostering connection and joy. Now, I hope to share the lessons and accomplishments I've gathered along the way, hoping my story may inspire and support others on their own paths.

Silent Strength

By Maureen Denise

For years, she poured her heart into her business, running a salon out of a rented building. Month after month, she paid rent, watching the money slip away like water through her fingers. And then, one day, a thought struck her like lightning—*Why am I throwing all this money away when I could own something of my own?*

The idea took hold of her, refusing to let go. It followed her into her dreams, whispering possibilities in her ear. But being self-employed was unpredictable. Some days were good, others slow. The financial risk loomed over her like a storm cloud. Still, she kept her faith. Somehow, the bills always got paid.

She turned to God, as she always did when faced with a big decision. "Lord, is this what You want me to do?" she prayed, seeking guidance, looking for a sign. And as she waited for an answer, she continued to envision it—her building, her salon, her dream coming to life.

But there was one problem.

She was married, and while she hoped this could be an investment for their future, her husband saw things differently. He never supported her career, never liked that she did hair. Time and time again, he told her to quit, to find something else. And when she dared to mention her dream of buying a building, his response was full of negativity.

So she moved in silence.

She stopped sharing her thoughts, even with friends and family. Instead, she prayed. And then, one day, while driving through a familiar neighborhood, she saw it—an abandoned house on a busy corner. She had passed it countless times growing up, but now, it looked different. Now, she saw potential.

Every time she drove by, she pictured what it could become. She imagined the changes, the transformation. The thought wouldn't leave her alone, so she acted on it. She found out who owned the property, picked up the phone, and called.

A kind woman answered.

With a hopeful heart, she introduced herself and asked if the owner would be interested in selling. The woman promised to ask her husband and get back to her. And so, she waited.

Weeks passed before the phone rang again. The answer was no. Her heart sank, but something deep inside told her don't give up.

So she kept praying.

Determined, she drove around town searching for other possibilities. Then, she found it—another house, right on a high-traffic street. And this one was for sale. Excited, she put in a contract and waited for the bank's response. She could already see her salon inside, already imagine the transformation.

And then, just as she was waiting for the bank's decision, the phone rang again. It was the woman from before. "My husband changed his mind," she said. "He's ready to sell."

Her heart raced. This was the property. The place she had prayed over. But she had just committed to another. Unsure of what to do, she told the woman she'd have to wait and see.

Then came the bank's decision. They declined the loan—the asking price was higher than the property's worth. Disappointed but not discouraged, she made one last attempt to talk to her husband about the first property. As expected, he had no interest.

So she followed her heart.

She called the original owner back and said she was ready. When she walked into the building for the first time, she knew—this is it. She could already see where everything would go, where clients would sit, where she'd create her dream.

And then, something incredible happened.

The owner handed her the key. "Keep it," he said. "Take your time, bring whoever you need to check things out."

She was speechless.

As they discussed the price, he revealed another surprise—the financing would go through him. No bank. No middleman. Just an agreement between them.

Still, there was one obstacle—the down payment. Ten thousand dollars. "I'm sorry," she said, "that's why I was going through a bank. They had programs to help with that."

The owner looked at her for a moment, then smiled. "Tell you what—I'll waive it." Her eyes filled with tears.

A week later, her uncle, a professional appraiser, offered to do an appraisal for free. It came back almost exactly at the price she had been quoted. Everything was falling into place.

At closing, another surprise awaited her. She only had to pay $200.

$200 to secure the building she had prayed for.

And if that wasn't enough proof of God's hand in her journey, the previous owner told her something else. "Don't worry about the first couple of months' payments," he said. "Take your time. Get your business transferred. Make sure everything is in order first."

She could hardly believe how it all unfolded.

With faith, prayer, and perseverance, she had done it. She owned her building. Her dream was no longer just a vision—it was real.

And despite the doubts, despite the naysayers, despite every obstacle, she knew one thing for sure—God had worked it all out.

A Leap of Faith: A Journey of Business, Love, and Self-Discovery

The moment had finally arrived. The doors to my business were opening, and everything I had envisioned was coming to life. Every room, every carefully selected piece of furniture, and every piece of equipment fit perfectly, just as I had imagined.

The grand opening was a day of celebration and blessings. My pastor came to pray over the building and the business, his presence filling the space with peace and encouragement. As he walked through each room, he gave me a thumbs-up and a warm smile. I was overjoyed, but what surprised me the most was my husband's reaction. He saw the pastor's approval, and for the first time in a long while, he seemed excited—perhaps because another man had recognized the accomplishment.

Business flourished over the years, even though workers came and went. I faced the challenges that came my way, always keeping things running. Through it all, I knew I was never alone. God was with me, guiding me, watching over me, making sure I had everything I needed.

But while the business was thriving, my marriage was crumbling. No matter how hard we tried, my husband and I could never seem to get on the same page. Slowly, I found myself feeling more connected to God than to the man I had vowed to spend my life with. Eventually, we parted ways and divorced. It was a painful transition, but even in that loss, I felt God's presence. Without my husband's help or support, I continued to push forward, and I was still blessed.

Then came the pandemic, a storm I never saw coming. Customers weren't coming in like before, and the beauty industry was shifting in ways I hadn't anticipated. The building, now older, began showing signs of wear. Water leaks crept into the walls, seeping into the wooden floors, threatening to weaken the very foundation of what I had built. But I didn't panic—I took care of it, just as I always had.

One day, in the quiet of my heart, I heard God speak: "I need you to get by yourself and focus on you."

I obeyed. And in that solitude, I discovered truths about myself that had long been buried beneath the noise of life. I decluttered— physically, emotionally, and spiritually. I let go of people who no longer served my purpose. I took self-love classes, sat still, and truly listened to what God wanted me to know. I realized that when God wants to speak, He often does so through the wisdom of others.

One day, a remarkable woman shared something profound with me. She suggested selling the building while the market was high. The words struck a chord deep within me because, unknowingly, my spirit had already whispered the same thought. I had always believed that my business had to be tied to that building, but God was showing me another way.

The building was aging, and maintaining it was becoming a burden. Though I had financed it for 20 years and had only four more years left before it would be fully paid off, I knew this was the right time. It was time to release and move forward.

I reached out to my realtor, and together, we listed the property. For three months, there was only one interested buyer. We negotiated back and forth, but we couldn't agree on the terms. Disappointed but not discouraged, I remained patient. Then, weeks later, the buyer called back, ready to meet my terms.

Excitement bubbled within me. God had worked it out again!

When the deal was finalized, I couldn't believe it—I had tripled my profits! What a blessing!

This journey had been one of faith, perseverance, and transformation. I had walked through seasons of success, heartbreak, struggle, and self-discovery, but through it all, one thing remained constant: God's presence.

And as I stepped into the next chapter of my life, I knew—without a doubt—that He had already paved the way for something even greater.

Stacey Dori

CEO of Gifted Administrative Services

https://www.linkedin.com/in/staceygarel/
https://www.facebook.com/stacey2qute
https://www.instagram.com/Iamstaceydori
https://www.giftedadministrativeservices.com/
Yourspiritualgoddess.com

Stacey Garel is an Bestselling published author with the 9 times best selling book Peeling Off The Layers To Unmask New Beginnings. She is also a natural born Prophetess. Stacey is originally from Atlanta, GA, residing in Stonecrest, GA DeKalb County. She is a certified Event Planner professional & writer. Stacey has been a dedicated expert of events for over 15 years working as a Director of Events & Tradeshows. Having worked on National conferences, trade shows, and events such as the 2012 DNC for former President Barack Obama & the 2013 & 2019 Super Bowl. In 2023 Stacey was nominated for a RICE Award as Founder's Rising Star. In 2023 she received and Outstanding Citizen Award from her home state of Georgia. Stacey is an active motional speaker & leader in her community. Her ultimate goal is to always be an inspiration to all she encounters.

Breaking Barriers in Corporate America: A Nice Girl's Journey to Triumph

By Stacey Dori

My Story

In a world where the expectations for women, particularly women of color, can feel insurmountable, my journey as Stacey Garel is a testament to resilience, tenacity, and the unwavering belief that nice girls can, and do, finish first. Growing up in America as a Black woman shaped my identity and instilled in me a fierce determination to succeed despite the obstacles I faced.

My story is one of overcoming adversity, breaking barriers, and ultimately claiming my place in a corporate environment that often felt unwelcoming. From an early age, I learned that life would not always be fair. My childhood was spent in a vibrant neighborhood where I was surrounded by family, friends, and a community that nurtured my dreams. My mother emphasized the importance of education and hard work, often telling me, "You have to work and pray for what you desire." These words resonated with me throughout my life, becoming a guiding principle as I navigated the complexities of adulthood.

In 2011, I landed an amazing job opportunity as an Events Manager at a prominent company. I was excited about the opportunity and eager to prove myself in a competitive environment. However, the reality of my situation quickly set in. The corporate world was not as welcoming as I had hoped. As the only Black woman in the office, I often felt isolated. The subtle microaggressions and overt discrimination from some of my colleagues were hard to ignore. It wasn't long before I began to experience bullying and harassment from higher-ups. The favoritism shown towards colleagues of other ethnicities was glaring. I watched as they received praise for their work, while my contributions were often overlooked or dismissed. Meetings that should have been collaborative turned into battlegrounds where my ideas were belittled. It was demoralizing, and I often found myself questioning my worth and abilities. Despite the challenges, I refused to let negativity define my journey. I leaned on my support system—friends, family, and mentors—who reminded me of my capabilities and encouraged me to keep pushing forward. They helped me recognize that my voice mattered, and I began to gather the strength to stand up for myself. I started attending workshops and networking events to build connections with other professionals who understood the unique struggles faced by women of color in the workplace.

One pivotal moment in my career came during a crucial presentation to a major client. I had poured my heart and soul into the event, meticulously preparing every detail. As I stood before the clients, I felt a surge of confidence. I knew that I was prepared, and I refused to allow the doubts planted by my colleagues to overshadow my abilities. The presentation was a success, earning praise not just from the clients but also from my peers. For the first time, I felt a glimpse of acceptance within my workplace. However, the journey was far from over. The pushback from my higher-ups intensified. I became a target for their insecurities, facing constant scrutiny and unfair criticism. I had to learn how to navigate these challenges with grace and intelligence. I started documenting every incident of sexual harassment, bullying, and discrimination, creating a paper trail that I hoped would protect me. It was during this time that I found solace in the stories of other Black women in my circle of friends and family who had faced similar struggles. Their triumphs inspired me to keep fighting. I joined a local organization dedicated to empowering women of color in business, where I found a community of strong, resilient women who shared their experiences and strategies for success. Together, we celebrated our victories and supported one another through the tough times. One of the most valuable lessons I learned through this organization was the importance of self-advocacy. I began to articulate my achievements more confidently, ensuring that my contributions were recognized. I scheduled regular meetings with my manager to discuss my progress and express my aspirations for growth within the company. I became an advocate not just for myself but for other women of color as well, speaking out against injustices and calling for a more inclusive work environment.

As I continued to assert myself, I also sought mentorship from women who had successfully navigated the corporate landscape. Their guidance was invaluable; they provided insights into strategies for overcoming barriers and offered encouragement during moments of self-doubt. I learned the importance of building a personal brand and leveraging my unique perspective as a Black woman in business. Over time, my hard work and resilience began to pay off. I received recognition for my contributions to successful events and was eventually promoted to a leadership role. This achievement was not just a personal victory; it symbolized the possibilities for other women of color aspiring to succeed in their careers. I made it a priority to uplift and mentor younger employees, sharing my experiences and encouraging them to voice their ideas and ambitions. Through all the challenges, I realized that my journey was not just about personal success; it was about paving the way for others.

I began organizing a support group within my company focused on diversity and inclusion, advocating for policies that supported underrepresented groups. I wanted to create an environment where everyone felt valued and empowered to contribute. As I reflect on my journey, I recognize that the obstacles I faced were not just barriers but opportunities for growth. Each challenge strengthened my resolve and deepened my understanding of the importance of representation in the workplace. I became passionate about advocating for change, working to dismantle the systemic issues that perpetuated inequality within corporate America.

In sharing my story, I hope to inspire other "nice girls" to embrace their strength and resilience. It's essential to understand that kindness does not equate to weakness. Being a nice girl means nurturing relationships, fostering collaboration, and lifting others as you climb. My journey taught me that while the road may be challenging, it is possible to succeed without compromising one's values. Today, I stand proud as a Black woman in a leadership position, ready to champion diversity and inclusion in every aspect of my work. I advocate for the next generation of women, encouraging them to embrace their identities and pursue their dreams unapologetically. I strive to create spaces where their voices are heard, valued, and celebrated. In the end, my journey is a reminder that nice girls can and do finish first. With determination, resilience, and the support of our communities, we can overcome obstacles and create a brighter future for ourselves and those who follow. As I continue to navigate my career, I remain committed to being a beacon of hope and change in the corporate world, proving that kindness, strength, and perseverance can lead to success, no matter the odds.

Lori Ellen Miller

Spiritual Empowerment Pathfinder & Soul Cartographer

https://www.facebook.com/lori.miller.9659283
https://allmebydesign.com/

Lori Ellen Miller is a Spiritual Empowerment Pathfinder, Certified Quantum Human Design Specialist, and creator of the Soul Cartography™ system. As the founder of Soul Journey Secrets, she guides spiritually aware women to reclaim their truth, transform emotional wounds into wisdom, and align with their Divine Design. Through personalized soul-mapping experiences, she helps women uncover the deeper meaning behind their soul's chosen path. Lori supports women in rising into their fullest expression—living, leading, and serving from the soul with their inherent gifts. Her work is rooted in intuitive insight, lived transformation, and fierce compassion. Lori's mission is to awaken women to the power within so they can embody their sacred path and fulfill their higher calling with clarity, confidence, and authenticity.

Rising Beyond Fear:
A Soul-Guided Step Toward Visibility

By Lori Ellen Miller

There was a time not long ago when the idea of recording a simple two-minute live video felt like standing on the edge of a cliff. My body reacted as though it was being pushed toward the edge—heart pounding, hands trembling, my throat tightening. On the surface, it made no sense. I had lived through far worse. But in that moment, fear gripped me in a way that was paralyzing. I had never experienced this before.

I had recently begun a new chapter—launching a business anchored in soul work and spiritual empowerment. I had clarity about my purpose, I had done years of inner healing, and I had a message I deeply believed in. Still, this small act—pressing "go live"—shook something inside me that I wasn't prepared for.

As I stared at the screen of my tablet, heart racing, a familiar shame crept in: *You should be past this by now.*

But healing isn't linear.

That moment of resistance cracked open something deeper. I could feel it. This wasn't just about a video. It was about visibility, voice, and vulnerability. It was about being seen. And as someone who had once learned to survive by staying invisible, being seen wasn't just scary—it was threatening to the old survival patterns still stored in my nervous system.

I tried to coach myself through it. I used every tool I knew: breathwork, affirmations, grounding practices. But the fear wouldn't budge. I felt trapped between the woman I was becoming and the young version of me who still believed that being seen wasn't safe.

The next day, the anxiety lingered like a fog I couldn't escape. I questioned everything: *Was I really meant to do this work? Could I lead others if I couldn't get past this moment?*

And then came the turning point.

In a moment of quiet desperation, I stopped trying to push through. I opened my palms to the sky, and with a trembling voice, I whispered to the Universe—my spirit, my soul, my higher self:

"If this is something I need to do, I need you to help me—because I can't."

It was a prayer. A surrender. A release of control. And almost immediately, something shifted.

Within fifteen minutes, a calmness began to settle over me. It was subtle but profound, like warm light washing through every part of me that had been clenched in fear. I didn't need to know where it came from. I just knew I wasn't alone.

I received a clear message—an inner knowing—guiding me to regulate my nervous system first. Not to fight the fear, but to hold space for it. To offer it presence. To listen to what it had to say without believing it.

That afternoon, I stepped in front of the camera again. I wasn't fearless, but I was anchored.

I hit record. I spoke from the heart. And for the first time, I smiled.

It wasn't perfect. But it was real. It was me.

And that was enough.

That moment became a defining shift—not just in my business, but in my being. It reminded me that courage isn't the absence of fear. It's choosing to trust your soul's voice louder than the echoes of your past.

I began to realize how many of us carry old wounds that still whisper doubts in moments of expansion. We mistake fear as a stop sign, when often it's simply an invitation to slow down and listen. To attune to the parts of us that want to feel safe before they can move forward.

What I learned that day is something I now share with the women I guide: Your fear doesn't mean you're broken. It means you're stretching. It means something sacred is awakening within you that doesn't yet feel fully held.

And the more I've honored that inner dialogue—the soul-led whispers, the trembling truths—the more I've witnessed my own voice become clearer, stronger, more grounded in purpose.

Now, I look back on that two-minute video not as a failure or a hurdle, but as a portal. It was the moment I chose to let love lead. It was the day I stopped demanding perfection and started honoring presence.

It taught me that visibility isn't about performance—it's about connection. It's about showing up as you are, trusting that your authenticity is the medicine someone else might be needing in that very moment.

Since then, I've gone live many times. I've spoken to groups. I've taught workshops. But I still remember that first trembling step— and I hold it with reverence.

Because every step we take toward our truth, no matter how small, shifts something in the collective.

We give others permission to rise. To be seen. To be real.

And that, to me, is sacred service.

So if you find yourself at the edge of your own visibility cliff, heart racing, voice shaking—I want you to know this:

You're not behind. You're not broken. You're being called.

And when you answer with presence, the next step always reveals itself.

That's how we rise.

One soul-led step at a time.

Buffy Olson

Fire Vinyasa by Buffy
Owner & Instructor

https://www.linkedin.com/in/buffy-olson-9a460a303/
https://www.facebook.com/share/1HRQiXXFPE/
https://www.instagram.com/firevinyasa_by_buffy
https://www.firevinyasa.com/

Buffy Olson is a 200-hour yoga instructor and holds certifications in Hatha, Meditation, Chair, Gentle yoga, and Trauma-informed yoga. She opened her Sole proprietorship, Fire Vinyasa by Buffy in January of 2021 and has since facilitated and guided weekly private and group yoga sessions. Although Yoga and Coffee is her true love, Buffy Olson holds bachelor's and master's degrees in development psychology and Mental and Public Health. She spent several years working in social services as a mental health professional in Montana where she grew up, met her husband, and had four children. Buffy and her family moved to Colorado in 2019. It was in Colorado that Buffy began to practice yoga and decided that the best way to support and empower people to heal, prosper, and achieve their best selves is through the holistic practice of wellness in which yoga plays a major role.

Becoming Fire Vinyasa

By Buffy Olson

When I was twelve years old, I stepped on the scale and watched the numbers spin. My siblings were all weighed in the range of 90 pounds, but my number stopped at 180. My dad looked up and, with shock in his voice, said, "Buffy, you're obese." The word began to penetrate my life. I buried my head into my mother's lap and cried, "I don't want to be obese," I sobbed. This moment set the tone of my adolescent and young adult life.

With my mother's help, I lost weight, weighing 130 pounds at age 16. But as I learned to drive, got married at 19, and had two children, my weight creeped up to 230 pounds. Again, I set out to lose weight, not wanting to hit 250. I did lose weight and continued to lose through two more pregnancies, this time getting down to 160 pounds. But then, after my fourth child turned two and I quit breastfeeding, my weight began to increase and I wasn't sure what to do or why, so I scheduled a doctor's appointment where I was told, and not kindly, that I was eating more than I realized and I needed to exercise more (my husband even came to the appointment to vouch for my eating habits), without being offered any real support. Feeling defeated, I slowly gave up trying, and my weight started going back up.

By 2018, my weight reached its all-time highest, 282, but I had also finished grad school and worked my way from youth advocate to Case Manager, and to Family Support Specialist but the almost 300 pounds on my 5'6" frame was wearing on my body: my hips hurt, my knees would get sore, and going up any incline or stairs made me breathe embarrassingly hard. I didn't want to focus on my weight. Since that doctor's appointment and the devastation of putting weight back on, I had committed to just enjoying my life in a fat body, but I needed to get healthier. But what changes could I make with the schedule I had? I decided on a few simple changes: no more frozen/fast food, and more walking. I began parking in the back of the parking lots and always taking stairs instead of elevators (something that still frustrates my family). That small but consistent change shed 20 pounds.

In 2019, my husband took a job in Denver, Colorado. I stayed at about 260 until we moved to Colorado.

My situation is not unique; the average woman in America is 5'4" and sedentary. According to *Women's Health*, a study done in 2012 by the Northwestern University of Feinberg School of Medicine found that most American women spend an average of nine hours a day sitting. We sit in our cars for work, many of us sit at a desk or with clients for several hours a day, then we sit while driving our kids to and from school and other activities, and we sit while picking up food for dinner. That doesn't leave a lot of time for movement. Most women are busy and hardworking but not expending a lot of physical energy. That is a combination for weight gain, diseases, feeling hungry, probably lacking important nutrients, and having an overall feeling of being tired and not feeling well or healthy.

I decided to take a break from working outside the home and focus on my family and health. The first couple of weeks, I lost some weight just walking up and down stairs throughout the entire day. Once the house was mostly in order, I made a commitment to walking at least two to three miles a day, no matter the weather or how I felt, I walked every day. And I started cooking healthier meals and counting calories. These changes helped me shed another 20 pounds.

By the time I saw a doctor in Colorado, I weighed 242 pounds, and in early 2020, COVID and the shutdown happened, so I decided to stay on my health journey. I added a 20-minute workout video from Jillian Michaels to my walking, and then I swapped Jillian Michaels for Chalene Johnson, my personal fitness and entrepreneur heroine.

I completed her Turbo Jam and PIYO workouts, and PIYO ignited a deeper interest. After PIYO, I signed up to become a licensed yoga instructor, and I became licensed in December of 2020.

Yoga was what really had the lasting changes in my life; I had done kickboxing and cycling, and I did get fitter and stronger with every workout, but yoga was the practice that taught me about myself. Through practicing yoga, I learned to meditate, to connect to my whole self. I learned to be present in my body to relax, to focus on myself, and to be okay in moments of discomfort, and to even stay in the moment. Not only did my body heal from yoga, but so did my mind and mental health. The benefits of yoga for physical and mental health are long and growing every day, but yoga is also one of the few fitness practices that changes body composition and reduces visceral fat. Yoga is a powerful tool that not only strengthens the body but eases stress and teaches important functions such as using your breath to calm oneself.

I also kept slowly tweaking my nutrition to slowly be healthier. One year later, I lost exactly 100 pounds from the time they saw me the first time, but I had lost over 100 pounds.

Throughout my year of weight loss, I thought a lot about what I was going to do. Go back to work in the same sedentary industry? As I contemplated, I thought about the day I felt things really changed, the real key to my success, and the underlining reasons for my weight gain and struggle throughout my life. I remember looking in the mirror in my new house knowing I had to start again, but I was so tired of not liking me, of feeling ugly, and never feeling like I was thin enough or pretty enough, so I looked in the mirror, I forced myself to study my own body (usually I would quickly turn away or cover up), but this time I decided I was going to find something about my body I liked and instead of working because of how much I disliked my body I was going to focus on improving something I already liked. That was it, it was the key! I quickly found that working on my body out of love bred more love; I found more and more about myself that I liked, and as I found more to like, the more progress I had. Before I reached my long-term goal, I had an appreciation and affection for myself. And I decided that's what I wanted to do; I didn't just want to teach yoga; I didn't want to go back to the work I was doing. I wanted to share the confidence, purpose, and healing I experienced through yoga with other women who have struggled as I had. I wanted to find a way to offer other women the support and healing they needed to find success.

I opened Fire Vinyasa by Buffy sole proprietorship in January of 2021, at first offering classes out of my second living room that I converted into a yoga studio. A part of the inspiration for the name came from practicing yoga in front of my fireplace in that room. I offered classes to anyone and anywhere: protein clubs, small groups of nurses, and other small groups charging 10 to 25 dollars per private or class until I managed to get enough experience to start getting contracts all over the Denver area. I started teaching yoga at places like the Gaylord and Hilton and offering classes at corporations like Oracle. The best thing about every class, from the small to the large, is when a woman tells me how much she needed the class, whether for the physical aspect or the mental aspect. My personal and business yoga practice is still maturing and finding purpose, but a guiding value of Fire Vinyasa by Buffy is to make yoga accessible to all, no matter their class or background, particularly women.

The goal of reaching more women and supporting them on their own journeys of becoming their best selves, whether that is emotional healing, self-confidence, or weight management, will always be a guiding light of Fire Vinyasa by Buffy, whether I'm teaching small or large classes, local or abroad. Wherever life takes me on this journey, the purpose is to reach others along their path with a supportive hand.

References:

Sengupta P. Health Impacts of Yoga and Pranayama: A State-of-the-Art Review. Int J Prev Med. 2012 Jul;3(7):444-58. PMID: 22891145; PMCID: PMC3415184.

(2019, July 2). Should Women Aim for 2,000 Calories a Day? The Final Say is In. *Women's Health*. https://www.womenshealthmag.com/uk/food/weight loss/a28241466/2000-calories-a-day/

Trish Lynn

The Trish Lynn
Coach

https://www.linkedin.com/in/trish-lynn-7306b9281/
https://www.facebook.com/profile.php?id=100071442180745
https://www.instagram.com/thetrishlynn

Trish Lynn is a dedicated single mom of three and a survivor of narcissistic abuse. With her journey from victim to victor, she has transformed her life into one of empowerment and purpose. As a content marketing strategist, Trish specializes in helping women who have endured toxic relationships regain their voice and thrive in business. Her mission is to inspire and guide others to reclaim their power and succeed in both their personal and professional lives.

From The Mud, We Can Create Beauty: Breaking Generational Patterns and Creating Success

By Trish Lynn

The Moment I Knew I Had to Break the Cycle

I was nine when I lost my dad to cancer, but I remember so many memory pieces from an early age. I saw control masquerading as love. My dad's voice boomed through the house, his presence taking up so much space that it felt suffocating. My mom, silent. My sister and I, frozen with fear.

As I grew up, I watched my grandpa do the same to my grandma. The same sharp words. The same tight grip. The same suffocating presence that made it seem as if this is normal.

My marriage, from the honeymoon stage to control in the snap of your fingers. But this was normal for me. So, I stayed. I did everything to bend without breaking, so he was happy, and my kids had a family that was whole.

And then, my sister. Her own relationship mirrored the same cycle we were raised in. The same fear. The same silence. The same weight of a life.

For so long, I thought this was just how life was for women. That love came with control. That success had limits. That my voice would always be something to shrink, not something to be heard. I was expected to be a yes girl. No voice, no opinion, no say. After all, I got to be a stay-at home mom. I needed to be grateful for everything he did for us.

But deep down, something in me knew this wasn't normal. And I refused to be another woman in my family who lost herself to a cycle she never asked to be part of. And I refused to let my daughter grow up thinking this was acceptable. One night after fighting all day, my ex was drunk and came to bed ready to fight. Told me to "do him and the kids a favour and kill myself." The switch flipped, and I was done. Already mentally and physically disconnected, now emotionally disconnected.

The Weight of Generational Patterns

I didn't just grow up watching toxic relationships, I grew up believing they were normal.

The control. The silence. The fear of saying the wrong thing at the wrong time. Always walking on eggshells. It was woven into my childhood, passed down like an unspoken rule: this is just how things are.

I watched my mom shrink herself to keep the peace. I watched my grandma do the same. And then, without even realizing it, I became that woman, too, second-guessing myself, making myself smaller, believing that love, success, and happiness had to come at a cost.

I carried the weight of generational patterns in ways I didn't even recognize at first.

"Women should just be grateful for what they get."

So I settled. In love, in money, in what I thought I was allowed to ask for.

"Success is for other people."

My ex always referred to my business as a HOBBY. If I signed clients, I was consumed by my business. He feared my success, so I believed it wasn't possible for me. So, I played it safe and stayed small.

"Speaking up only makes things worse."

So, I silenced myself, even in my own business, afraid that if I was too much, too bold, too me, there would be repercussions.

These beliefs weren't mine, but I carried them like they were. And for a long time, they kept me stuck, until I made the decision that it ends with me.

Because if I didn't break the cycle, I'd pass it down. To my kids. To my daughter, to my boys. And I refused to let that happen.

The Breaking Point

I remember the exact moment I knew, *this cycle ends with me.*

It wasn't dramatic. No big explosion (well, on my end). Just a quiet moment of "I'm done."

I saw the way my daughter was being silenced in her opinions, already learning to shrink herself. I saw the way my sons watched, absorbing everything, understanding that love was control, manipulation was acceptable, and silence meant safety.

The fear of staying the same, staying in that environment, was bigger than the fear of changing.

For years, I told myself I wasn't ready. That I didn't have the money, the strength, the *right* circumstances to leave. But if I kept waiting for the perfect moment, I'd be waiting forever.

So, I made the decision to leave. It took me two months to find a place. Two months of moving from my son's bedroom (he had the biggest room) to my daughter's bedroom, sleeping on a single mattress on the floor.

And it wasn't glamorous. It was terrifying. Survival mode didn't magically disappear, I had to fight through it every single day. Severe anxiety that led to panic attacks. My mind, fighting me every step of the way.

Starting over meant unraveling every belief that had kept me stuck. It meant learning how to trust myself, how to stand on my own, how to create a life that didn't revolve around fear.

It meant building something *entirely* new, for me and for them.

And that's when I realized: I wasn't just breaking the cycle.

I was rebuilding everything and showing my kids a new way.

How Women Hold Themselves Back

Women don't hold themselves back because they lack potential. They hold themselves back because they were conditioned to believe their power is a threat.

When you've spent years walking on eggshells, shrinking yourself, and making sure everyone else is comfortable, success doesn't feel safe; it feels dangerous.

This is what trauma does. It wires your nervous system for survival, not success. It teaches you that being too much, too loud, or too visible comes with consequences.

So, you play small. You stay small.
You undercharge because receiving more feels unsafe.
You overthink every post, every word, because what if someone judges you?
You hold back because you believe that your voice doesn't matter.

I see it in the women I work with every day. They are brilliant, powerful, ready—but they hesitate. They say, "I just need more confidence," or "I need a better strategy," or "I need permission to be myself."

But it's not confidence.

It's not a strategy.

It's not external permission.

It's the deep, subconscious fear of what happens when they finally take up space.

And if this is you, I want you to know: You are not broken. You are conditioned.

Conditioning can be undone.
Safety can be rebuilt within your body.

You don't have to prove your worthiness. You don't have to wait until you "feel ready." You just have to decide that you are done living in the version of yourself that was built for survival.

Because thriving isn't about doing more. It's about becoming the woman who is no longer afraid to own her power.

How to Step Into Power

Leaving a toxic relationship isn't just about walking away, it's about unraveling the version of yourself that was built to survive in it. It's about realizing that the woman you had to be to endure that chapter is *not* the woman who will build the next one.

For years, I was stuck in survival mode. Believing that stability, no matter how suffocating, was safer than the unknown. But survival is not the same as living. And I realized I couldn't spend another moment as a woman who was only half alive.

This is identity work at its core. That wanting more, more money, more freedom, more peace, was selfish.

The beliefs I carried weren't mine. It was *given* to me by him, so slowly I didn't even realize it.

But the moment I decided to break the cycle, everything changed.

Not instantly. Not easily. But step by step.

The shift from surviving to thriving isn't just about making more money or growing a business. It's about becoming the woman who *can* hold more.

Who can be seen without fear.
Who can charge her worth without guilt.
Who can trust herself to create the life she actually *wants*.

Because this was never just about business. It's about reclaiming my voice in *every* area of life.

It's about saying *no* to relationships that drain me.
It's about demanding more than *barely enough*.
It's about finally fully owning who I am.

I built my business, my freedom, not because I had all the answers, but because I refused to keep living in a story that wasn't mine.

Break the Cycle

Right now, you're standing at a crossroads.

One path is familiar. Safe. It's the version of life you were *taught* to accept, one where you keep playing small, doubting yourself, waiting for permission to take up space. It's a path built on survival, not freedom.

The other path? It's unknown. Uncomfortable. It requires you to become someone your past wouldn't recognize. To stop settling. To stop waiting. To *stop apologizing* for wanting more.

Leaving a toxic relationship and breaking generational patterns isn't easy. But neither is staying stuck.

You weren't meant to carry the weight of old stories. You weren't meant to shrink yourself so others feel comfortable.

You are here to break cycles, not repeat them.
To rewrite the narrative for every woman who comes after you.
To create a life built on *your* terms.

You are not here to repeat history. **You are here to change it.**

Erica Elliott

WarriorHeart Healing Hearts
Counselor, Coach, Speaker, Consultant

https://www.linkedin.com/in/erica-elliott-ms-lpc-b90911150
https://www.facebook.com/warriorheartxo
https://www.instagram.com/warriorheartxo
https://msha.ke/warriorheartxo
https://linktr.ee/WarriorHeartxo

I possess a Master's Degree in Counseling Psychology and have invested over three decades in my career as a Licensed Counselor, Certified Brain Health Coach, and Certified Health Integrative Medicine Professional as well as military and medical experience. My expertise encompasses a broad spectrum of therapeutic approaches, such as Neurobiology, ADHD and Neurodiversity, Somatic Therapy, Energy Medicine, Neuro-Linguistic Programming (NLP), Cognitive Behavioral Therapy (CBT), Rational Emotive Therapy (RET), Emotional Freedom Techniques (EFT), Thought Field Therapy (TFT), Theology, Eye Movement Desensitization and Reprocessing (EMDR), the Gottman Method, alongside Mindfulness and Meditation. I am an Author and Entrepreneur and I love connecting with people! I am a wife, mom, and grandmother with a zest for adventure and trying out new things. My daughter and I own a social media marketing company where we feature businesses. I am the owner of WarriorHeart Healing Hearts where I champion a comprehensive healing philosophy that harmonizes the mind, body, and spirit. I am the founder of Energetic Elevation where I help people clear up the Mess to discover their MASTERPIECE! Over the years, I have had the honor of empowering thousands of individuals to heal, grow, glow and soar! Having faced my own set of adversities and emotional challenges, I understand that true healing flourishes within the framework of compassionate connections. Together, we nurture resilience and vitality, transforming our own legacies and those of future generations. Like iron sharpening iron, our collaboration fosters a profound healing journey. If you're looking for support or just want to connect I'd love to hear from you! Be Blessed and Be a Blessing!

Elevating Kindness: Fostering Profound and Impactful Relationships

By Erica Elliott

Life often unfolds in unexpected ways, providing us with rich lessons that shape who we are. For me, some of the most important insights came not from formal education or structured teachings, but rather from the unique experiences that have marked my journey. Growing up in a family where positive communication was lacking, I navigated my formative years without the benefit of influential movements or the modern technology that connects us today. The environment I grew up in was devoid of many conveniences that are now commonplace, such as the internet and mobile devices. Yet, despite these limitations, I discovered a profound truth: the importance of surrounding myself with people who bring positivity, encouragement, and support into my life.

As a teenager, I made a conscious decision to seek out relationships that were uplifting and nurturing. I understood that even if my circle was small, the quality of those connections mattered far more than their number. There were times when I felt isolated and longed for deeper connections, but my belief in treating others with kindness and respect guided my choices. I learned that while some relationships needed to be let go, I didn't have the skills to do that in a healthy way, so I adopted the workaholic skill to create what I thought at the time was healthy. Today, I know that was avoidance, which only leads to other problems along the way.

After completing my formal education, I gained a deeper understanding of what constitutes healthy and unhealthy relationships. I developed skills that allowed me to recognize the qualities that foster positive connections and those that can lead to toxicity. This newfound knowledge not only empowered me personally but also ignited a passion within me to share these insights with others. I wanted to foster this awareness in my children, equipping them with the tools to navigate their own relationships more effectively.

A particularly memorable moment stands out that encapsulates these lessons. I recall a time when my daughter came home after spending time with a group of friends. One of the girls in her group had taken another friend's phone and began teasing her about her weight. My daughter, witnessing this hurtful behavior, took action. She approached the girl, took the phone from her, and firmly stated that such behavior was not OK. In that moment, I experienced a swell of pride as a mother, realizing that my daughter had found the courage to stand up for her friend.

However, this proud moment was quickly followed by a difficult conversation. We had to discuss whether my daughter should continue trying to maintain a friendship with the girl who had behaved poorly, as this incident was not the first of its kind. This was a challenging discussion, especially since the girl was considered one of the popular kids—beautiful and charismatic yet engaging in behaviors that were clearly unhealthy. I emphasized to my daughter the importance of making her own decisions rather than having them made for her. I wanted her to understand that establishing boundaries is not only acceptable but necessary. If someone chooses to act unkindly, it's perfectly okay to step away from that relationship and seek out connections that are more supportive and healthy.

There were also other instances where my daughter faced friends who would gossip or stir up issues with her other friendships. We navigated similar tough conversations in those situations as well. I reminded her that the right friends would remain in her life, actively working to build healthier and more fulfilling relationships alongside her. This mutual investment is what ultimately fosters strong and supportive bonds.

Today, I am proud to say that my daughter has blossomed into a remarkable young woman who runs her own business and is surrounded by an incredible group of friends. These friends are loving and supportive, always lifting each other up. For any parent, I cannot stress enough the importance of teaching children how to cultivate healthy relationships, helping them understand what behaviors are acceptable and what should not be tolerated.

My husband and I have faced similar challenges with our son, who has also had to make tough decisions about friendships that weren't beneficial for him. Leaving a relationship, although it may seem daunting at the moment, is not the worst outcome. The true worst-case scenario is becoming more like that person or allowing oneself to be mistreated and taken advantage of. This is why it is often said that you become like the three to five people you spend the most time with—the influence of our closest relationships can profoundly shape who we are.

Reflecting on my journey as a mother, I felt a deep responsibility to share the lessons I had learned over the years with my children. I wanted them to grasp the essential tools of healthy communication and the importance of self-worth—lessons that I had to discover through my own struggles with codependency and a desire to please others. Growing up within a strict Christian framework, I often misinterpreted the teachings of love and kindness, unintentionally allowing myself to be taken advantage of in the name of faith. It was only by confronting and healing from my childhood wounds of abandonment and rejection that I gained the strength and clarity needed to foster healthier, more fulfilling relationships.

The first step in any healing journey is recognizing the need for change. After my previous marriage ended, I sought counseling with renewed determination, concentrating on the attachment issues that had affected my relationships throughout my life. I realized that understanding what I truly wanted from my connections was vital.

By articulating my vision for healthy relationships, I learned to establish firm boundaries and define what was nurturing and acceptable in my life. Today, I can say I have amazing, positive, healthy friendships.

It's essential to recognize that our upbringing significantly influences our perceptions of what is normal. However, it is equally important to critically evaluate these norms and consider whether they serve us well in the present. Cultural influences and family dynamics can create patterns that may not be beneficial. For instance, during my childhood, expressing emotions was often discouraged, while relentless hard work was praised and rewarded. This contradiction contributed to my struggles with workaholism and emotional suppression. I was committed to teaching my kids and clients the importance of balancing ambition with emotional intelligence—an understanding I had to develop later in life.

Here are twelve guiding principles that I believe foster healthy relationships, which can serve as essential reminders in our interactions with others:

Healthy Relationship Skills

1. **Open Communication:** Engaging in honest and transparent discussions fosters a culture of openness and understanding.
2. **Active Listening:** Valuing and respecting others' perspectives by listening attentively without interruption shows genuine care.
3. **Mutual Respect:** Honoring each other's boundaries, opinions, and individuality strengthens the bond between individuals.
4. **Conflict Resolution:** Addressing disagreements calmly and constructively promotes a focus on solutions rather than blame.
5. **Supportiveness:** Encouraging each other's dreams and aspirations while providing emotional backing strengthens resilience.

6. **Trust Building:** Creating an atmosphere of honesty and reliability cultivates a profound sense of security in the relationship.
7. **Healthy Boundaries:** Understanding and respecting personal space and limits fosters mutual comfort and understanding.
8. **Equality:** Ensuring collaborative decision-making empowers both individuals and promotes a sense of partnership.
9. **Empathy:** Striving to understand and validate each other's feelings nurtures deeper connections and trust.
10. **Quality Time:** Valuing moments spent together enhances intimacy and strengthens emotional bonds.
11. **Flexibility:** Being willing to adapt and compromise shows consideration for each other's needs and preferences.
12. **Positive Reinforcement:** Regularly expressing appreciation and affection enhances overall relationship satisfaction.

Unhealthy Relationship Skills

1. **Poor Communication:** Frequent misunderstandings can lead to emotional distance and disconnection over time.
2. **Dismissive Listening:** Ignoring or interrupting others' feelings breeds resentment and disengagement.
3. **Disrespect:** Undermining or belittling each other's worth creates a toxic dynamic.
4. **Escalation of Conflict:** Arguments that lead to hostility can damage the foundation of relationships.
5. **Lack of Support:** Dismissing aspirations fosters feelings of neglect and isolation.
6. **Distrust:** Secrets and dishonesty breed suspicion and insecurity in relationships.
7. **Overstepping Boundaries:** Disregarding the need for personal space leads to feelings of suffocation.
8. **Imbalance of Power:** When one person dominates decisions, it creates feelings of helplessness in the other.

9. **Lack of Empathy:** Failing to recognize each other's emotions fosters disconnection and alienation.
10. **Neglect of Time Together:** A lack of quality time creates emotional distance and feelings of loneliness.
11. **Rigidity:** Resistance to change stifles growth and understanding.
12. **Negative Criticism:** Frequent insults create a toxic environment and diminish self-esteem.

I encourage you to reflect on these principles with an open heart and a sense of curiosity rather than harsh self-judgment. Identify the areas where you excel and those that could benefit from further development. Often, individuals exhibiting aggressive or anxious behaviors are grappling with their own insecurities. Understanding that these traits stem from past experiences can foster compassion and empathy rather than condemnation.

Throughout my extensive career as a counselor and coach for over thirty years, I have witnessed the transformative power of choice and self-awareness. Each individual has the potential for meaningful change, but only if they are willing to embark on a journey of self-discovery and growth. I am profoundly grateful to be a part of the She Rises community and the She Wins global network, where we uplift and empower one another in impactful ways. Together, we can create a nurturing environment that promotes growth, healing, and shared success.

Every one of us possesses the remarkable ability to change our world for the better. Let us embrace this journey together as we heal, grow, glow, and soar! I help people clear the mess to discover their MASTERPIECE! Imagine soaring in your life's purpose and abundance as you dive deep in my Masterpiece God Centered Mastery Coaching Course using the 777 Method God gave me to clearly soar in life. Be Blessed and be a Blessing!

Corinne Brown

Corinne Brown Coaching
Leadership/Results Coach

https://www.linkedin.com/in/corinne-brown-36513673/
https://www.facebook.com/corinnebrowncoaching
https://www.instagram.com/corinne_brown_coaching/
https://corinnebrowncoaching.com

Corinne Brown is a resilient leader, life coach, and advocate for personal empowerment who transforms adversity into strength. Drawing from her experiences surviving a toxic marriage and workplace harassment, Corinne has dedicated her life to helping others rebuild their confidence, overcome challenges, and thrive. With 14 years of leadership coaching expertise, she empowers individuals to embrace resilience, self-worth, and emotional intelligence to lead with authenticity and purpose. Corinne's coaching programs, including her popular "Mindset Reset" series, inspire transformation through clarity, reframing, and actionable strategies. She is a featured speaker at national and international summits, co-author of She Stands Strong, and her story is highlighted in Becoming an Unstoppable Woman. Through her contributions to She Wins, Nice Girls Finish First, Corinne redefines leadership, proving that success and kindness are not mutually exclusive but rather the ultimate power duo. Her tip for resilience: focus on small, consistent actions to build strength.

Becoming Unshakable

By Corinne Brown

There was a time in my life when I believed that kindness meant acceptance, that loyalty meant reciprocity, and that deep friendships were unbreakable. I thought that if I gave my all, if I showed up, supported, and loved without conditions, I would receive the same in return. Not so!

I lost friendships I thought would last forever. I was gaslit into doubting my own reality. I was shunned, left wondering what I had done wrong when, in truth, I had only been myself, caring, giving, and unwilling to play games. And yet, through the heartbreak and betrayal, I discovered something far greater than I had lost—my own power.

This is my story of loss, resilience, and the unwavering truth that nice girls don't just finish, they win.

The Breaking Point: When Friendship Turns to Betrayal

I can still remember the day it all shifted. What had once been a deep, trusted friendship slowly turned into something I no longer recognised. The warm conversations became laced with subtle jabs. The inside jokes felt more like private mockery. The support that had once been freely given now came at a cost, one I was unwilling to pay.

At first, I dismissed the signs. I convinced myself that I was overthinking, that maybe they were just having a bad day. I ignored the gut feeling that told me something wasn't right, because I wanted so badly to believe in the people I had let so deeply into my life.

But gaslighting works like that, it makes you question your instincts. It makes you doubt your own reality.

The people I once called my closest friends began rewriting our history. Suddenly, the support I had given was forgotten, the memories we had built together erased. I found myself cast as the villain in a narrative I didn't recognise. And no matter how much I tried to seek clarity, to understand what had gone wrong, I was met with silence. With exclusion. With a carefully orchestrated campaign of whispers and cold shoulders.

I was being shunned. And it hurt in a way I had never experienced before.

The Tell-Tale Signs: When Friends Start to Ghost and Isolate You

Looking back, I can now see the signs that my so-called friends were slowly pushing me out of the group. At the time, I wanted to believe it was all in my head. But the pattern was clear. Here are the red flags I wish I had paid more attention to:

1. **Conversations Became One-Sided** – They stopped asking about my life. Whenever I shared something personal, the conversation would quickly shift back to them or die out completely. I started feeling like an outsider in my own friendships.

2. **Plans Were Suddenly "Forgotten"** – I would hear about get-togethers only after they had happened. When I asked why I wasn't invited, I was met with dismissive responses like, "Oh, I thought you were busy" or "It was last-minute."

3. **Group Chats Went Silent, For Me** – The group chat, once full of daily messages, suddenly went quiet, except, I later found out, there was a new one. One that didn't include me.

4. **They Stopped Tagging or Including Me in Social Media Posts** – It might seem trivial, but when you're the only one not tagged in a group photo or you notice that your friends

are hyping each other up online but never acknowledge you, it stings.

5. **Inside Jokes Became Weapons** – They would laugh about things I had no idea about. When I asked, they would say, "It's nothing," as if I had become a stranger overnight.

6. **Their Energy Shifted** – The warmth was gone. Conversations felt forced. When I entered the room, I could feel the shift, like I had walked into something I wasn't supposed to hear.

7. **They Stopped Defending Me** – When others spread rumours or twisted the truth about me, my so-called friends stayed silent. Or worse, they joined in.

8. **I Was Always the One Reaching Out** – I was the one texting first. The one making plans. The one holding on. And when I stopped trying? Everything fell apart because I was the only one keeping it together.

Each of these signs on its own might seem small, but together, they paint a clear picture. I was being phased out, ghosted, and isolated. And no matter how much I tried to salvage those friendships, the truth was, they had already decided I no longer belonged.

The Pain of Isolation: When the World Feels Smaller

Losing friends is never easy, but losing them to manipulation, false narratives, and deliberate exclusion is devastating. It forces you into an emotional freefall, questioning everything you thought you knew about yourself.

Was I too much? Was I too nice? Did I deserve this?

The silence was the worst part. The way people who once laughed with me, confided in me, suddenly acted as though I had never existed. No confrontation. No explanation. Just a void, where once there had been a connection.

It's in these moments that self-doubt creeps in like a shadow. I began replaying every conversation, searching for my mistake. I wanted closure, an apology, something to make it all make sense. But the truth is, not all betrayals come with explanations. Sometimes, people remove you from their lives not because you've wronged them, but because they can no longer manipulate or control you.

And that's when I realised, this wasn't about me. It was about them.

The Turning Point: Choosing Myself

The day I decided to stop seeking validation from those who discarded me was the day I started winning.

At first, the grief was unbearable. It felt like mourning, because in a way, it was—I was grieving the friendships I thought I had, the people I believed would always stand beside me. But with that grief came an awakening.

I started reflecting on the patterns, on the small red flags I had ignored. I realised that I had been surrounded by people who thrived on control, on subtle put-downs, on competition disguised as camaraderie. I had given my heart to those who only knew how to take.

And when I finally set boundaries, when I chose to prioritise my own peace instead of chasing people who had no intention of being in my life, I found freedom.

She Wins: The Power of Resilience

Winning doesn't always look like revenge or proving people wrong. Sometimes, winning is simply refusing to let broken relationships break you. It's choosing joy despite the pain, growth despite the setbacks.

I rebuilt myself, piece by piece. I found strength in solitude, in the quiet realisation that I was whole all along. I redefined my circle, filling it with people who saw my kindness not as a weakness, but as a strength. People who didn't need me to dim my light so theirs could shine.

And here's what I know now:

- **Nice girls don't finish last, they finish stronger.**

- **Kindness isn't a weakness, it's a power few truly understand.**

- **Boundaries aren't walls, they're gates that let the right people in.**

- **Being shunned is painful, but it's also a gift; it reveals who truly belongs in your life.**

I no longer chase friendships. I no longer question my worth based on who stays or who leaves. I stand in the truth of who I am, knowing that the right people will recognise my value.

So to every woman who has ever felt the sting of betrayal, the loneliness of exclusion, the heartbreak of losing people who never truly saw her, know this: You are not alone. You are not broken. You are not too much.

You are a force. You are resilient, and you will rise. Because nice girls don't just finish.

They win.

Carol Salvadori

Founder of LeadLoud Academy
Empowerment Coach

https://www.linkedin.com/in/ube/
https://www.facebook.com/leadloudacademyofficial
https://www.instagram.com/leadloudacademy/
www.leadloudacademy.com

Carol Salvadori is the Founder and Empowerment Coach at LeadLoud Academy—a transformative platform dedicated to helping individuals discover and harness their true voices. With a foundation in corporate environments, Carol honed skills in leadership and strategic thinking before co-managing a successful wine bar bistro. This unique blend of experiences allowed her to master the balance between business acumen and personal aspirations. Inspired by her own transformative journey, Carol pursued professional coaching certification and launched LeadLoud Academy to foster resilience and authenticity. Today, she passionately inspires her clients to leverage their unique strengths and embrace authentic leadership. Carol's mission is rooted in the belief that employing one's authentic voice is the most powerful tool for achieving true joy and lasting impact.

Promises of Strength: A Journey from Heartbreak to Hope

By Carol Salvadori

From the moment my daughter Lilli entered this world, she has been my guiding light—a beacon through the darkest of nights and the brightest of days. Her captivating blue eyes, mirroring the vastness of the ocean, held within them a truth I found undeniable: the boundless possibility and the power of love. It was this love, pure and steadfast, that became the foundation upon which I built my journey of transformation and resilience.

Even before Lilli was born, my world began to shift. During those months of anticipation, I immersed myself in learning, driven by the desire to offer her the best start in life. Each day was filled with reading, classes, and quiet moments of reflection, envisioning the life I wished to nurture. I promised myself, and her, that I would strive tirelessly to provide a world filled with warmth, opportunity, and unconditional love.

As part of this dedication, I vowed to write Lilli a letter each year, capturing moments and milestones with the ink of love and keen observation. These letters became more than expressions of affection; they were chronicles of a journey shared between mother and daughter, marking each new chapter of her life with written memories. So cherished were these missives that later, she began her own tradition of writing—a practice she embraced as a form of gratitude and connection, and that she treasures to this day.

In the early days, our lives revolved around the rhythm of our wine bar bistro—a shared vision with my husband as intoxicating as the finest vintage we served. Under the warm glow of ambient lights, we navigated the complexities of business and family life, finding moments of harmony amidst the hustle. The bistro was more than a livelihood; it was the backdrop to our family's story, a place where dreams were nurtured, and memories made with each exchanged smile across the bar and every toast raised in friendship.

Yet, amidst the comforts of routine, a profound yearning began to stir within me, calling during those quiet moments alone in the garage. Under the guise of simple tasks, like cooking, where the familiar aromas filled the air, this feeling transformed into a meditative state. Here, with each slice and simmer, my heart echoed with dreams of purpose and fulfillment that seemed ever elusive. In those moments of reflection and yearning, Lilli's presence was ever persistent, described by others as an invisible circle she instinctively sensed.

This circle was so profound that even when she was engaged deeply in play, absorbed in her world, my crossing its boundary was instantly noticed. I recall instances when a simple task, like stepping out to do laundry, was met with her youthful urgency, calling my name or seeking me out—her trust a comforting constant in a life that would soon change unpredictably.

Then life, with its unpredictable storms, intervened. One day, like a tremor felt through the earth, my husband announced he was leaving. Yet, even amidst such upheaval, our shared commitment to Lilli's well-being remained resolute. Our separation and subsequent divorce were approached with an amicable understanding that Lilli and her emotional security took precedence. We told her as a family, inviting her into an honest circle of truth where she could ask questions, express emotions, and understand that her parents' love for her remained boundless.

I remember that night, standing over Lilli as she slept, her chest rising softly with each breath. In that moment of serenity, amidst my own swirling chaos, I promised her, whispered into the stillness, that we would not only survive this storm but emerge stronger, thriving.

The ensuing days were an emotional whirlwind, each decision fraught with uncertainty. I moved us to new environments, believing a change of scenery might bring the peace we sought, though geographical changes proved to be fleeting in their relief. A return to familiar grounds became necessary, where responsibilities awaited, and life's familiar rhythms could resume their course.

Back on familiar soil, I resumed work in positions that offered financial stability but little else. The monotony starkly contrasted the unresolved emotional turmoil within. Each task felt like a performance; my true feelings concealed beneath a practiced facade meant to preserve Lilli's sense of security. Yet, I knew in my heart she sensed the undercurrents—her intuitive nature picking up on the shifts our lives undertook.

Simultaneously, Lilli began confronting her own battles at school. Her radiant nature drew both admiration and unfair scrutiny, presenting challenges she faced with quiet strength. Her resilience amidst such trials provided a mirror to my own challenges—a catalyst needed to chart a new course in life.

Determined to reshape our lives, I sought guidance from a life coach, marking the beginning of significant transformation. Through each session, tightly held beliefs were unravelled, revealing the fundamental truth that self-love was not indulgence but necessity. This realization was heartening yet formidable, a climb towards self-forgiveness and renewal.

The journey towards self-discovery was not undertaken alone; Lilli's presence was an ever-present source of inspiration. Her warmth and curiosity prompted me to pursue certification as a Life Coach—a role through which I sought to help others navigate the labyrinths of their lives. My time in Melbourne offered a fertile field for transformation, where camaraderie and shared experience cultivated growth and understanding.

Reflecting on my bond with Lilli, her trust in me provided strength in ways both large and small. Our mutual resilience became a mantra of empowerment, one that affirmed—"A strong woman stands up for herself. A stronger woman stands up for others." Together, we embraced this truth, our journey cemented by the twin forces of love and determination.

Each challenge faced together was a stepping stone, a testament to the route we navigated with honesty and courage. Embracing vulnerabilities transformed them into strengths, allowing our shared path to flourish, with resilience and hope as our companions. In sharing our story through *She Wins: Nice Girls Finish First*, we resonate with the endurance embodied by women worldwide, reminding us that through authentic narratives, personal triumph is redefined.

Today, with a clarity afforded by our journey, I am compelled to share our testament—one that underscores love's transformative power and resilience's capability to transcend adversity. Our story serves as a guiding light, inspiring others who seek their truth amidst the turmoil, and illustrating that those invisible bonds, fortified by love, are the keystones of lasting empowerment.

Even now, Lilli's journey continues to illuminate paths unexplored. Now in her 20s, she stands on the cusp of her own stories, armed with the letters that have charted our beautiful and complex journey together. They are reminders that in love there is strength, in resilience there is power, and in each other, we find the courage to weather any storm. As she ventures forward, embracing her own truths, I am reminded daily of the lessons we've crafted songs in the symphony of life that ring with resilience and joy.

Together, we hold fast to the belief that challenges are but gateways to growth and that each step taken in love pushes us ever closer to our most authentic selves. Through our shared experiences, may those who read our story be inspired to capture their faith in the light of love, confident that no matter the darkness encountered, the dawn of new beginnings is always within reach.

Jen Rigley

Founder of Flourishing Over Fifty®

https://www.linkedin.com/in/jenrigley/
https://www.facebook.com/flourishingoverfifty
https://www.instagram.com/flourishingoverfifty/
https://flourishingoverfifty.com/

Jen Rigley is an author, motivational speaker and personal transformation expert focused on women's empowerment and living your best life after 50. Her mission is to inspire and empower women in midlife to create a new story for their life, especially after facing significant challenges and trauma. Formerly a top sales and marketing executive working with both start-ups and Fortune 500 clients, Jen is the founder of Flourishing Over Fifty®, a brand whose powerful message is rooted in overcoming adversity in midlife. With years of real-life experience encountering and overcoming significant trauma and challenges Jen is sought after to share her story of resilience and triumphing over adversity. As a well-respected leader in women's empowerment, Jen inspires thousands of women to overcome challenges, heal and flourish in midlife through her Flourishing Over Fifty® community and her Flourish Journey Framework™.

Collaboration Beats Competition Every Time and Creativity Wins Out

By Jen Rigley

Most of my 30-year professional career has been in the male-dominated technology field, which I entered right after graduating from college. And so it often is in male-dominated arenas, there was not only intense pressure to succeed, but to succeed at the expense of others. There was constant competition, and it wasn't unusual to be berated or screamed at when projects went over budget or fell behind—as they so often did.

The entire business model was "up or out." This meant that you needed to progress every year in a significant manner, or you were invited to find a new role somewhere else. In this environment, there was no talking about family, personal life, or having a family. Women were provided with examples of what to wear, which was a man's suit but with a skirt instead of pants. We even had little bow ties that mimicked men's ties.

This is the environment I was trained in, and I found myself taking on those traits of aggressiveness so I could fit in and compete with everyone else. This dominant energy also seeped into my home life. I lost my softness, some of my kindness, and also lost track of my feminine side. I found it very difficult to transition from the workday to home time.

When I started thinking about having children, I realized I would be instantly sidetracked into a non-essential role at this company, and I made the decision on my own to find a new role that would hopefully provide a more supportive environment where I could have success at the office but at the same time be able to nurture not only my family but myself. I wanted to reclaim my kindness, my softness, my feminine side. I wanted to be surrounded by collaborative colleagues, not aggressively competitive colleagues.

It was then that I joined a female-led start-up where I was exposed to a whole new style of management and leadership. This company was no less assertive in pushing for the best performance from each team member, but the process and delivery were completely different. Instead of the "up or out" philosophy, it was encouraged to forge the path that worked best for you and for others in a collaborative method. When issues arose, we would discuss them and talk through ways to resolve—no tyrannic screaming to "just fix it," and most importantly, there were no more pointing fingers and accusing someone of making a mistake. Yes, the error or mistake was acknowledged, but in a "what can we learn from this" and not a "you might be fired" way.

I instantly felt these new styles of working seeping into me, like a sponge. At first, I would react as I was trained to react. It starts with a tightness, where stress and anger start to build up, and you're looking for whom you can place blame on. It happened in one of my first meetings at the new company, and as I felt those feelings arise, I could also feel at the same time that an outburst just wouldn't be appropriate in this setting. I was able to watch, listen, and learn as the founder walked through a collaborative process that we would use to find the root cause of the problem (not the "who caused the problem"), how we would create a timeline to resolve the issue and most importantly, how we would have a call with our client to discuss the issue and the resolution—calmly and without placing blame. This was such a game-changer: in the past, I had been in situations where we would be telling the client that we would be firing the person that caused the issue (even when it wasn't always clear what or who may have caused the issue, or it was a multitude of errors, not just one person).

It was that first day in my new role that I decided I was going to readjust my leadership style to fit with the company's style. Kindness and collaboration were my new modes of working. It was then that my sales performance really took off; I developed a unique selling style—collaborative, consultative sales. I took the time to get to know my client personally, I took the time to understand their key challenges, and then I took the time to craft a solution, or a proposal, for how our products and services could solve their problems. We worked in tandem, collaboratively, to create the best possible solution, which, of course, was always a more effective, creative solution.

I found that it was in taking the time to really know my potential client, to understand their needs, and layering on the personal relationships that helped me become a stand-out leader in sales. It didn't stop there. Once the sale was made, I made sure to stay in touch and hold regular meetings to touch base. Did we discuss project status and sometimes difficult, challenging issues? Yes. But I also made time to ask about how they were doing, how their children were doing. I always led with caring, kindness, and collaboration, but followed through with making sure the job was done.

We don't have to beat our chests and tear down the guy next to us to be successful, even in an extremely competitive environment like sales.

The next time you find yourself stressed about a difficult conversation or making that sales call you've been dreading, try this instead:

Before you interact, center yourself. This is a simple yet powerful daily practice:

1. Stillness – Sit in silence, allowing yourself to quiet your mind and throw off the stress surrounding the possible outcomes.

2. Gratitude – Reflect on the things you are grateful for related to this conversation; it may be as simple as that you are grateful that you will be able to have the conversation.

3.   Intention – Set a meaningful intention for your interaction. A specific goal is good, but surround that with words that set the stage for your discussion so you enter it with positive, calm energy.

By dedicating three minutes to this practice before jumping into your sales call or difficult conversation, you will feel yourself shedding old ways of interacting. You will begin to shift your perspective, to move beyond stress and start thinking about an outcome that helps meet your goals but also those of the other person...whether it's personal or professional.

Once you have centered yourself, begin centering your client using the sensory modality of hearing, touch/feeling, and sight. This is a way to center true collaboration and leads to a more effective, creative solution.

What does the person on the other end of the phone or table need to hear, need to feel, need to see?

- They need to hear that you are listening to what they are saying, that you understand their needs, their fears, and their project goals.
- They need to feel that they can trust you.
- They need to see that you are being authentic.

Over time, you'll find yourself naturally approaching challenging situations in this collaborative manner, and the conversations and solutions will become more creative. Collaboration beats competition every time, and creativity wins out—and your success will follow.

Scan the QR code or follow the link to join the Flourishing Over Fifty community, receive a free gift, and take your first step towards the life you truly deserve.

SCAN ME

https://bit.ly/hannaselfcare

Follow on Social Media to get your daily dose of inspiration:

https://www.facebook.com/flourishingoverfifty
https://www.instagram.com/flourishingoverfifty/

Lacy J. Hardman

Founder of Swell Retreat

https://www.linkedin.com/in/hardmanrealtors/
https://www.facebook.com/SwellRetreatUtah/
https://www.instagram.com/swellretreat/
https://www.swellretreat.com/

I'm Lacy! I can't wait to get to know you! A bit about me: I jumped out of airplanes for 12 years while serving in the Army; I grew up in a very tumultuous home with a bi-polar mom; In the pursuit of happiness, I dedicated years to uncovering its root and can't wait to share my tools with you!!

My mission in life is to help others know they aren't alone on their journey, provide healing through the wisdom of horses, and overcome limiting behaviors. When a person decides to heal they prevent future generations of suffering.

As part of my work, I lead retreats, mentor emerging entrepreneurs and coaches, and host an APP called F.R.E.E.E., which offers courses on healing and connects people to horse retreats worldwide. Additionally, at Swell Retreat, I host family reunions, youth groups, and corporate groups. Speaker. Change Advocate. God-Loving.

The Weight Beneath the Weight

By Lacy J. Hardman

I realized I hit the "freshman 15" when I saw a recent photo of myself during college. At first, I didn't even recognize who I was. I thought it was someone else. But when I took a closer look, it hit me—it was me. I always had a round face with plush cheeks, but now it was really round, my thighs were putting so much pressure on the seams of my pants, ready to burst any moment, and there it was—a muffin top spilling over my waistband, something I'd never had before. My mom was always weight-conscious, and I couldn't believe that I had slipped from my own consciousness and let this happen. I felt panicked and desperate to lose it—and lose it fast!

The more I thought about it, the more I wanted to learn self-control so I could escape the cravings and lose the shame when I gave into them. Where had my self-control gone? I never had a problem with overeating. What changed? Why had I become my own worst enemy in the pursuit of my health goals?

Fast forward a year, I went on a weight loss journey, but still felt cursed! I've tried every diet—calorie counting, low carb, weight watchers—you name it. I worked out so much my sneakers were demanding overtime pay. So why was I still carrying around this "limited edition" muffin top and round face? I must have been genetically programmed when I turned 19 to store snacks in my thighs. "Honestly, it feels like I'm failing some cosmic fitness test. Hello, Universe, I'm doing all the things! Can I get a refund on these bad genes?!" Despite working out five days a week, I was still overweight. Each gym session felt like a small victory, but it always ended in defeat when I got home and couldn't resist the urge to binge on chocolate almonds, candy bars, and other calorie-packed foods, leaving me frustrated and full of shame.

I was in the Army National Guard at the time, and I had to get "taped." That's what they do when you're over the weight limit...when you are too heavy, according to their standards...when you are fat. They check your body fat index as a backup test to see if they need to put you on a special program. My heart sank as the sergeant pulled out the measuring tape. My palms were sweaty, and my face felt like it was on fire from the humiliation that had crept up from my neck. I stood there, frozen in place. How could I have done this to myself? When she wrapped the cold tape around my neck, I wanted the ground to swallow me whole. It wasn't just the tape—it was the sinking feeling of failure tightening around me like a rope.

This destructive cycle left me feeling trapped, ashamed, uncomfortable in my clothes, and increasingly worried about the toll it was taking on my health with weight gain and the looming risk of serious issues like diabetes or heart problems. Why couldn't I succeed? Why couldn't I break free from this pattern and finally shed the weight, for good? What if I did actually get diabetes or follow the footsteps of my dad and end up in open heart surgery? What if they kicked me out of the Army for being fat? I couldn't face that embarrassment.

Thankfully, I "made tape," but still, I never wanted to have that experience ever again. I could work out and I enjoyed working out, but I couldn't figure out how to stop giving in to my cravings and overindulging.

I had the opportunity to attend Army training to become a dental technician. I went to the training at Fort Sam Houston, Texas, and met a dentist there who had moved to the States from India. He had been compelled by the September 11th events to join the U.S. Army. He was smart, flirty, and we began to hang out after class. I began to lose the weight I had gained, and I wasn't trying to do anything different. But I no longer had a craving to indulge.

I ended up deploying to Afghanistan and had some really hard experiences there, reserved for another book. After this deployment,

I broke up with my dentist boyfriend; we had been having a long-distance relationship since we graduated training, and he wasn't willing to move to Utah, and I wasn't willing to move to New York. While deployed, I just realized that this was no way to live and let him go.

Several months went by, and the weight was coming back. I was still working out and "trying" to diet, just to have the diet be sabotaged by my own lack of self-control. I was lonely again and had lost touch with my high school friends after Army training and deployment. I had recently begun going to church, and I was praying to meet a new friend to connect with in this new chapter of my life. A couple of weeks later, one of my ROTC friends introduced me to his buddy who had just arrived home from serving a church mission.

We started spending every spare moment together. Then, he got a job on campus, and I got to see him even more. Over time, I noticed something unexpected—my face looked slimmer in a photo, there's the girl I used to know. Curious, I stepped on the scale in the campus locker room, and there it was—I had lost the weight I'd been carrying for so long. But here's the strange part: I hadn't even been trying. No diets, no obsessing over calories. It just happened. How?

Eventually, we got married. It was wonderful—until it wasn't. The cracks appeared, and soon, we divorced. I found myself single again, and slowly, the weight crept back. The cycle began again, like a loop I couldn't escape. Over the next few years, I swore not to fall into another serious relationship. Instead, I focused on friendships, trying to keep things simple. And once again, as I surrounded myself with connection, the weight started to melt away.

But the pattern became undeniable. Every time I was in a relationship—romantic or just deeply connected—the weight would come off. Yet, when I was alone, no amount of workouts or dieting could stop the scale from climbing back up. It wasn't about food or exercise anymore; it was something deeper. The weight seemed tied to my emotions, to the state of my heart.

Why did my body respond so strongly to a connection? Why did loneliness bring back the heaviness, both physically and emotionally? I couldn't figure it out, but I knew one thing for sure: this wasn't just about pounds or calories. This was about something far more painful and profound.

It took me nearly a decade to uncover the true root of my patterns of overeating and even the root problems that led to my divorce. Surprisingly, the answer didn't come from my years of talk therapy or countless attempts at body-focused healing. It came from a horse. Watching the raw, instinctual behavior of a wild horse and the conditioned responses of a trained horse during their interactions with a trainer opened my eyes. It revealed the deep connection between the mind, body, and brain in a way I'd never understood before. After that experience, I dove deeper into research, I had another epiphany that my pain was from my childhood rather than the present moments of overeating. I wasn't my own worst enemy, sabotaging my own goals. People caused me pain in my youth, and I needed to heal from that. I took a lesson from the horses and got curious. I learned to be nice to myself, invested time in understanding myself and healing my emotional wounds.

Emotional eating is more than just snacking when you're bored or indulging in comfort food after a long day. It's a pattern driven by deeply ingrained emotional triggers, often rooted in childhood experiences, unresolved trauma, or unmet emotional needs.

In my case, I uncovered that my emotional eating stemmed from an insecure attachment with my mom. Growing up, I lacked a quality connection with her, which left me feeling emotionally unfulfilled. Food became my substitute for love and connection—the one thing that filled the void, even if only temporarily.

This isn't unique to me. Research has shown that emotional eating is often linked to underlying emotional wounds, and one of the behavioral symptoms is a reliance on external sources of comfort, like food, to regulate emotions.

I created Hearts and Horses with my husband. It's a signature system that gets to the root cause of your overeating, or any other sabotaging patterns that keep you from achieving your goals. It can save you thousands in therapy and dieting costs, and reduce the emotional turmoil of feeling like a failure or your own worst enemy.

Discover the path to self-love and lasting happiness. Hearts and Horses can help transform your life, bringing peace and joy to every aspect of your journey. Take the Pattern Quiz now to see your patterns—and join us, either in person at Swell Retreat or online with Live Swell. Your breakthrough starts here!

She Wins: Quiz

Carmen K. Maendel

Nate's Property Maintenance LLC
Co-Owner & Business Office Manager

https://www.linkedin.com/in/carmen-maendel-17510944/
https://www.facebook.com/ncmaendel/
https://www.instagram.com/maendelcarmen/
http://natespropertymaintenance.com

Who is Carmen K. Maendel? I am a child of God, a wife, and a mother. I have owned and operated 4 businesses (Genoa Denim & Leather Apparel, Carmen Maendel Photography, and Maendel Fitness Gym & Spa) in the last 12 years and currently am Co-Owner/Business Office Manager for Nate's Property Maintenance LLC. We are a husband wife team! I handle all the business stuff on the home front, and my husband, Nate Maendel coordinates everything on the job sites with our clients and crew. Nate has over 30 years experience with removing and trimming trees of any size and shape! Nate is also five star approved through Home Advisor/Angi. With over 30 years of expertise, we specialize in tree removal, trimming, and total property transformations. Year-round tree work, free estimates, and a passion for serving our community make us your go-to for a beautiful, safe outdoor space. Nate & Carmen.

We Desperately Need Jesus

By Carmen K. Maendel

Introduction: Nice Girl or Mean Girl?

Hello friend, I am Carmen Maendel, and I am a child of God. I am not perfect, only Jesus can be perfect! I make mistakes, mess up, make wrong judgment calls, jump to conclusions, have miscommunications, disagreements, and generally am what you call "flaw-some". I am full of flaws and awesome at the same time. I am perfectly imperfect! I am created in God's image, and I am exactly how He designed me to be. I also love to uplift, encourage, bond at a deep level with, walk alongside both women and men, and experience life with them as God intended us to do! I am incapable of surface-level friendships in my life because of how God has designed me to be. I have very few deep-level friendships in my life with a plethora of acquaintances. My husband, Nate Maendel, is my closest and deepest soul-friendship connection and understands me like no one else on this earth. I am both a nice girl and a mean girl at the same time! There is an explanation for this in my upcoming narrative I am about to share with you!

The Middle School Debacle

I don't think middle school is easy for anyone. I remember this time very clearly in my mind, and it has helped shape me into the Godly woman that I am today. This is what I remember about middle school. I remember issues with female friendships and boys and the confusion of it all, simultaneously. I remember how everyone, including myself, was striving so hard to fit in that at any expense we would put others down in order to feel good about ourselves. I remember one thing very clearly at that time of my life. My horse, Ed, was my number one best friend, and he was loyal one hundred percent of the time. I remember coming home from school in tears nearly once or twice a week, and jumping on my horse, bareback, to run to the end of our property line. There were numerous stories told to my big, beautiful black Tennessee Walker at that time in my life. This period of time helped me grow thicker skin and become more resilient to many other life experiences I have had since then. I developed coping strategies for myself, and a unique approach to lifting up and encouraging both women and men. At this point, I was both a nice girl and a mean girl for pure survival mode in middle school; however, I was leaning toward nice! By starting to take the focus off myself and placing it on others, I was able to feel empowered in various scenarios.

Discovery of the Fruits of the Spirit

College life and entrance into corporate America presented their own set of unique and precarious challenges. I experienced power struggles with both men and women, and a deep appreciation for differing views and interpretations of life at the same time. I was beginning to get a taste of and practice the Fruits of the Spirit before I even knew they existed. Love, Joy, Peace, Patience, Kindness, Goodness, Faithfulness, Gentleness, and Self-Control. God has provided many situations that I have had the ability to learn and practice the Fruits of the Spirit in my life. One experience I had was when I was still working as a Financial Advisor and Stockbroker that sticks out in my mind. I was kind of a mean girl and quite full of myself at this point in my life. My husband today refers to that time in my life when I was a "highfalutin" stockbroker. I admit it, I was a brat. I cared very little about other people and mostly about the profits I was making at the bank where I was working at the time. I drove my JAG, wore a three-piece suit, and had my hair up in a bun; I played the part well. I was a "top banker," financial advisor, and stockbroker, and made more money than any of the other bankers at that branch at that time. My co-workers were fed up with me and conspired to devise a devious plan to get me out of the bank. This was the plan: they would wait until no one else in the bank had a license high enough to help a client with a stocks and bonds investment but me. I was the only licensed banker who worked there with a Series 7 Stock Broker license. All the other bankers I worked with just had their Series 6 and not a Series 7 license. Then, they would have me help Nate Maendel (who at that time in my life was simply a friend of mine and nothing else) with his investments over the lunch hour. They then later brought me into the main office to speak to the corporate over the phone, more like interrogating me. I asked to have my attorney present, and they denied my request. They falsely accused me of helping a "family member" with an account at the bank, which would be an extreme conflict of interest; however, Nate Maendel (at that time in my life was not a family member to me). They were successful in falsifying information and falsely accusing me of a Code of Conduct violation on my perfect, spotless U4. After consulting with my attorney, I put in my "resignation in lieu of termination" request shortly thereafter, and God removed me from my successful eight-year career in this field. Little did I know at the time that God was using Nate, my husband today, as a conduit to draw me away from a life and future filled with extreme materialism and idolatry. Directly following my leaving the bank, my life would take on a very different trajectory, embracing deep spiritual meaning and peace. In retrospect, several years later, after rededicating my life to the Lord on November 4, 2006, I approached one of my former co-workers from the bank, apologized for my despicable behavior back then, and asked for their forgiveness. It was a moment of mutual forgiveness for both of us, and peace was restored between us. We both won!

I also was given the opportunity to practice a full array of the Fruits of the Spirit when I owned my own gym and spa, Maendel Fitness. I loved how God would present various situations that He gave me the opportunity to have patience and kindness towards my clients. I was able to form deep connections with over fifty women at the time that I owned and operated our gym. Every day was a lesson not only for my clients, but for me as well in love, gentleness, and self-control. I learned more about life in general during that period of time than at any other time in my life. I was deeply connected to God and my clients, and prayed for guidance and direction to help my fitness and nutrition clients break through all types of barriers. I remember working with specific clients for a year or so and developing such a deep bond, level of trust, and respect in each other that was insurmountable. I attribute all the success of my clients directly to my obedience to following the plan that God guided me to take. I spent those eight years deepening my relationship with God and my clients simultaneously. It is bittersweet as I look back upon those days of fellowship and incredible growth and success with my Maendel Fitness and Nutrition clients. I knew exactly when to push and when to draw back a little, ensuring the highest sense of achievement in their programs. I knew this because I listened to God and followed the plan He laid out for me to train my clients. I always encouraged my clients to never compare themselves to anyone except themselves. I always said, "Aim at being a better version of yourself today than you were yesterday!" God guided me with the perfect mix of the Fruits of the Spirit to help me mirror and match, encourage, push, and facilitate my clients to a higher level of fitness than they had ever had before. I am able to use this epiphany to learn, lead, and work with our clients today with Nate's Property Maintenance LLC.

This brings me to today, working with Nate's Property Maintenance LLC. I definitely have achieved and have more of an abundance of peace in my life as a nice girl rather than a mean girl. There is so much truth to the saying, "You can catch more bees with honey than with vinegar." Nice girls really do finish first. My husband and I have multiple opportunities each day to exercise the Fruits of the Spirit with our clientele. I believe God has a sense of humor and will give us multiple scenarios with the same "fruit" to see if we finally get it.

Nate and I have both been humbled in multiple situations in business and our personal life. I am always quick to give grace, mercy, and forgiveness because I know that someday the tables may be turned, and I may be the one seeking the grace, mercy, and forgiveness from someone else. The more I try to put myself in someone's proverbial shoes, the more I have a deeper sense of empathy and love for that person. I have also realized that the thing that bothers me most about someone else is usually an underlying issue that I have not dealt with in myself. The Golden Rule always applies when working with my husband, our NPM Team, and our clients: "Do unto others as you would want them to do unto you."

I have included tips and tricks to being a nice girl and getting along and empowering others in both your personal and business life in the second half of this chapter, "We All Desperately Need Jesus" of the book *SHE WINS: Nice Girls Finish First*. When we "win" in life, everyone "wins" as we continue to lift up, encourage, speak truth and positivity, motivate, walk alongside, and empower other women in our lives!

Nice Girl Attributes and Characteristics (28 Things I Have Learned in My Life)

1) Be Not Susceptible to Petty Jealousy

Jealousy can cause trust issues and insecurity in relationships, hindering both personal and mutual growth.

2) Be Dependable

A quality woman is true to her word and follows through after she promises to do something.

3) Be Honest

Honesty is a valued trait and plays a crucial role in every area of our lives.

4) Be Forgiving

Forgiveness is an attribute of strength, and holding a grudge only harms you and not the other person.

5) Be Kind and Compassionate

Treat everyone with respect, be empathetic to their pain, and help them in any way you can.

6) Be Positive

A quality woman has a positive outlook on life and does not perseverate on their problems.

7) Be a Good Listener

Be an excellent communicator and pay full attention to someone when they speak.

8) Be Funny and Entertaining

Be cheerful and lighthearted to help lighten up stressful situations in life.

9) Be Humble

Take constructive criticism to heart, accept your flaws, and work daily to improve yourself.

10) Be Supportive and Motivating

Support and encourage those around you to achieve their dreams.

11) Be in Charge of Your Life

Accept responsibility instead of making excuses and own up to your mistakes in life.

12) Be Respectful of Yourself and Others

Value and love yourself before you expect the world to do the same to you.

13) Be Responsible and Hardworking

Work diligently and responsibly to achieve your goals.

14) Be Independent

Don't rely on anyone outside of God for your happiness.

15) Be Loyal

Be faithful, stand up for what you believe in, and don't break trust with anyone.

16) Be Patient

Be patient and wait upon the Lord, and don't worry or complain during the process.

17) Be Fun and Energetic

Know when to let your hair down and have fun while you are achieving your goals.

18) Be Genuine

Stick to your authentic self and personality, and don't try to impress others around you.

19) Be Dignified

Respond to everything in a grown-up and dignified manner.

20) Be Aware and Steer Clear of Gossip

Do not speak badly about others behind their back, and stop someone from talking negatively about someone else.

21) Be Accepting of Your Imperfections

Don't look down on others, and encourage them to be a better version of themselves.

22) Be Open to Expressing Yourself

Have the courage to express yourself and open up to others you trust.

23) Be Ambitious

Setting and achieving goals, with God's guidance, gives purpose to your life.

24) Be Mindful of Your Health and Self-Care

Take care of yourself and your body while you are busy helping everyone else out as well.

25) Be Diligent About Choosing Your Circle of Friends

Choose your friends carefully because you become who you hang around, and reduce toxicity from your life.

26) Be Teachable and Knowledgeable

Always be open to learning new things and hearing different opinions from others.

27) Be Courageous

Have a strong will, speak up, and do not be afraid to say "no" to something that goes against your values.

28) Be Trustworthy

Be honest, genuine, keep your promises, and be approachable for those that trust and confide in you.

Lovely LaGuerre

Pure Heavenly Hair and Beauty Boutique
Wealth Creator, Best Selling Author & Strategies Coach To Thrive In
Life and Business

https://www.linkedin.com/in/lovelylaguerre/
https://m.facebook.com/pureheavenlyhairboutique
https://www.instagram.com/pureheavenlyhair
https://www.lovelyinspireyou.com
http://www.pureheavenlyhair.com
https://lovelysellsvegas.com

Lovely LaGuerre is a Wealth Creator Amazon Best Seller and a Business Strategist.

Lovely leads life with purpose and believe in leveling the plane fields in business and in personal life. Keep thriving in your business and collaborate with like minded individuals.

Having An Unstoppable Woman Mindset Lovely shares her story that will inspire, motivate, and empower you.

Lovely is on a mission to help others to thrive in their business and building their legacy.

She's also the Founder/Owner of Pure Heavenly Hair & Beauty Boutique, a luxury beauty brand that will transforming, inspiring, and empowering women to unleash their beauty inside and out.

Lovely has a passion for supporting and empowering other women. She believes that together women can become unstoppable by leveraging their potential and giving back to their communities. She is a member of CALV, NAR, and LVR Association, and many more.

Additionally, Lovely is mission is looking to collaborate on podcast series dedicated to motivating and empowering women, through sharing their journey with other fellow female entrepreneurs. She is a member of CALV, NAR, and LVR Association, and many more.

Kindness as a Superpower

By Lovely LaGuerre

When I first entered the world of business, I was told that being "too nice" would be my downfall. I heard it all: You need to toughen up, people will take advantage of you, and kindness doesn't belong in the cutthroat world of entrepreneurship.

At first, I believed them. I put on a mask of cold indifference, thinking it was the only way to get ahead. But deep down, I knew this wasn't who I was. My values, my integrity, and my compassion weren't weaknesses, they were my strengths. And What I didn't know then was just how powerful kindness could be in creating success.

My story isn't just about starting a business; it's about rewriting the narrative of what it means to win as a woman in a world that often pits us against one another. It's about proving that you don't have to sacrifice your authenticity to achieve greatness. And most importantly, it's about showing that being kind and compassionate can not only open doors but also break barriers.

Rising Above Challenges

Growing up, I was taught that kindness was the foundation of every meaningful relationship. But when I stepped into the world of business, I quickly realized how rare this mindset was. Early in my career, I faced countless challenges. I started my first venture with little more than a vision and a determination to succeed. I didn't have investors or an extensive network, just a deep belief in my purpose.

I remember one particularly challenging moment when I pitched my business idea to a potential partner. I was met with skepticism and doubt. They told me I wasn't "cutthroat enough" to thrive in the competitive market. It was a pivotal moment for me. I could have conformed, tried to play by their rules, and hardened myself. But instead, I doubled down on what made me unique. I let my passion, my kindness, and my vision speak louder than their doubts.

It wasn't easy. I faced rejection, criticism, and setbacks. However, I also learned that every "no" brought me closer to the right "yes." And when that "yes" finally came, it wasn't just about the opportunity it was about the validation of staying true to myself.

Kindness as a Superpower

In a world where competition often takes precedence over collaboration, I made a conscious choice to lead with kindness. I treated my team, clients, and even my competitors with respect and empathy. I built relationships based on trust, not transactions. And slowly but surely, people began to take notice.

One of the most significant turning points in my journey came when I decided to mentor a young woman just starting her career. She had the passion, but lacked the confidence to chase her dreams. By pouring into her, offering guidance, and showing her that she had what it took, I not only helped her grow but also reminded myself of the power of uplifting others. She went on to achieve incredible success, and the ripple effect of that one act of kindness continues to inspire me to this day.

What I've discovered is that kindness isn't just about being nice, it's about showing up with integrity, listening with intent, and creating an environment where everyone feels valued. It's about turning competitors into collaborators, seeing challenges as opportunities for growth, and believing in the collective power of lifting others.

Breaking Barriers

As a woman in business, I've often found myself in spaces where I was underestimated or overlooked. But instead of letting that discourage me, I used it as fuel to push harder, dream bigger, and shatter the glass ceilings above me.

I once attended a high-stakes networking event where I was the only woman in the room. The atmosphere was intimidating, and I could feel the weight of being outnumbered. But instead of shrinking back, I leaned into my authenticity. I shared my story, my vision, and my passion with unwavering confidence. By the end of the event, I had secured two partnerships that became instrumental in scaling my business.

That moment reinforced a powerful lesson: You don't have to change who you are to fit in. Sometimes, being the outlier is your greatest strength.

The Power of Community

One of the most rewarding aspects of my journey has been building a community of like minded women who share my vision. Together, we've created a space where kindness and collaboration thrive. We celebrate each other's wins, support each other through challenges, and prove that success isn't a solo journey it's a collective one.

Through this community, I've seen firsthand how transformational growth can be. I've watched women rise above adversity, break barriers, and achieve dreams they once thought were impossible. Their stories inspire me every day and remind me that we're all stronger when we lift one another.

Triumph Through Perseverance

Success doesn't come without setbacks, and I've had my fair share. There were times when the pressure felt overwhelming, when self-doubt crept in, and when I questioned whether I was on the right path. But every challenge taught me something invaluable.

I learned that resilience isn't about never falling, it's about rising every time you do. I discovered that failure is just a stepping stone to success. And most importantly, I realized that staying true to myself, even in the face of adversity, was the key to unlocking my full potential.

Today, as I reflect on my journey, I'm filled with gratitude not just for the successes, but for the lessons learned along the way. I've built a thriving business, forged meaningful relationships, and created a legacy that I'm proud of. But more than anything, I've proven that being "nice" is not a weakness, it's a superpower.

A Call to Action

To every woman reading this, I want you to know that you have the power to rise above any challenges. You don't have to compromise your values to succeed. You can be kind, compassionate, and true to yourself and still emerge victorious.

Your journey won't be without obstacles, but every setback is an opportunity to grow. Every "no" brings you closer to the right "yes." And every act of kindness creates a ripple effect that can change the world.

So, let's rewrite the narrative. Let's prove that Kindness is a Superpower, nice girls don't just finish first they lead with purpose, inspire with passion, and create lasting change. Together, we can break barriers, shatter stereotypes, and show the world that kindness is the ultimate path to success.

When Women Rise We All Rise!

Charel Morris

Stone Circle Productions
Event Producer

https://www.linkedin.com/in/charel/
https://www.facebook.com/profile.php?id=61565048890800
https://www.instagram.com/cybershaman/
https://www.cosmicquantumshaman.com/home

Charel Morris is a seasoned event producer who found her professional calling in the tech conference world after twenty years in film and television production. Born and raised in Hollywood, California, she credits her father for teaching her the art of storytelling, a skill that has served her throughout her diverse career. Charel's journey from audio technician to respected event manager includes over two decades with DEF CON and mixed in ApacheCon and Black Hat, where she has helped guide these influential tech gatherings through years of tremendous growth. Her unique approach combines technical expertise with spiritual insights gained through her extensive work with shamanic teacher Lynn Andrews. In her chapter for "SHE WINS: Nice Girls Finish First," Charel shares how maintaining strong ethical boundaries and standing firm against manipulation led her to unexpected professional fulfillment. Her story demonstrates how authentic leadership and unwavering principles can create success while staying true to one's values.

Finding My Path: A Journey of Decisive Moments

By Charel Morris

One fateful day in the late 1990s, while waiting outside a sunny café in Beverly Hills, I noticed two women reading a book by Lynn Andrews, my favorite author and someone I worked with closely, managing her spiritual retreats around the world. Being naturally social, I leaned over toward their table.

"Do you like the book?" I asked, gesturing to the well-worn copy.

"Yes! I just finished it," one replied enthusiastically. "Her writing is incredible."

"Would you like to meet Lynn?" The words left my mouth before I'd fully considered them, something that happened often—intuitive offers that opened unexpected doors.

After a brief introduction—Lynn was always gracious with her readers—the women prepared to leave. As they stood, one handed me her business card. "I'm a meeting planner. I'd love to talk sometime." I slipped the card into my pocket, thinking nothing of it. In Los Angeles, everyone was always networking.

Weeks later, she called with an unusual request. She'd connected with someone running a "hacker conference" called DEF CON and had investors wanting to broadcast it live on the internet. Given my TV production background, could I put together a proposal?

"They want it running 24/7, like MTV," she explained breathlessly. "The money guys think it could be huge—broadcast worldwide."

This was 1999. The dot-com bubble was inflating rapidly, but streaming video wasn't what it is today—networks were just figuring out how to broadcast NFL games reliably. I knew cameramen who worked on MTV shoots and tech pioneers getting

ESPN streaming live. I crafted a proposal that accounted for every detail: broadcast-quality cameras, editing bays, union crews working round-the-clock, satellite uplinks, and the substantial infrastructure to make it all function seamlessly.

When the meeting day arrived, I flew to Las Vegas. The meeting room had that hotel blandness—beige walls, patterned carpet, fluorescent lighting that flattened everything it touched. As the investors launched into their vision, a disconnect became increasingly obvious. They spoke of millions of viewers while making references to technical specifications they clearly didn't understand. Meanwhile, DT—the conference founder—gave me subtle looks suggesting his skepticism.

When there was a pause, I spoke up. "I've never actually seen how this will look. What's the user experience like?"

DT smiled. "It's about an inch and a half square in the corner of your screen, usually a dark, fuzzy gray. And there's already a group streaming it for free."

I handed out my proposal and opened to the budget: $684,000 plus contingency. Their expected $25,000 projection evaporated like desert rain. So did they—vanishing without goodbyes, leaving their abandoned proposal binders like tombstones marking the death of ill-conceived ambitions.

My "friend" also made a hasty exit.

Left alone with DT, we both chuckled at the absurdity. As he described his community of hackers and technology enthusiasts, I found myself authentically interested. His passion was evident as he talked about creating a space where people could share knowledge freely. He invited me to come see DEF CON firsthand—he'd cover my expenses.

A few weeks later, after finishing a shamanic retreat in California, I flew to Las Vegas. That evening, watching attendees and volunteers setting up and connecting with each other, I had a profound realization: I'd found a new community. One I wasn't looking for, but somehow, I was home.

The energy was electric—people excitedly discussing ideas, sharing discoveries, solving problems together. Despite the technical nature of their conversations, I recognized the same human elements I'd found in every creative team: passion, collaboration, and the joy of creating something together.

My so-called friend had somehow maneuvered herself into becoming the meeting planner for both DEF CON and Black Hat, a more corporate-focused version of DEF CON. What became clear quickly was that she was mainly focused on finding men rather than ensuring events ran smoothly. She brought me in at minimal pay so she could be poolside meeting men, leaving me to handle the logistics.

There were other problems with her business practices. I often found myself caught between misleading clients or getting screamed at because she couldn't get money when she wanted it. Hotel staff came to me with questions she should have handled, contracts contained errors creating liability issues, and speakers were left without clear information. I stayed because I frankly liked our clients and felt responsible for ensuring their events succeeded.

After a couple of years, things came to a head during a particularly stressful setup. We were preparing for a conference, and I knew she was getting significant pushback from the client's board. She stormed into our office, face flushed with anger, and deliberately "bumped" my shoulder very hard. It wasn't exactly a hit, but the energy behind it was unmistakable—an attempt to physically intimidate.

I turned to face her, standing my full height—I'm about four inches taller. "Do not ever hit me again," I said firmly, my voice calm but resolute. I followed her into the hallway and informed her that I

QUIT—effective immediately. If she needed to communicate with me, it would be by text only—I no longer trusted her word.

Once back home, she requested to meet. Over coffee, her demeanor had completely changed. She apologized profusely and acknowledged that I was holding her top clients together. Would I please finish the year? She promised to stay out of the way during the conferences. After consideration, I increased my fee substantially and agreed to specific terms.

The first conference came weeks later. True to her word, she was scarce. But that night, after the first day had concluded, the president of their board found me.

"We're going to fire her," he said bluntly. "The board vote was unanimous. Would you step in and take over permanently?"

I wanted to say yes immediately—I loved working with this organization. But I held firm to my principles about not undermining others professionally.

"You need to complete your firing of her first," I told him. "Once that's done, ask me again."

They did their part, handling the termination professionally, and I worked with them for seven years afterward, creating profitable events for both their organization and my company.

Then, a few months later, I was in Amsterdam for my first European Black Hat conference. After checking into the hotel, I ran into DT in the lobby. He asked if I would have coffee with him.

"Do you have any contracts with her? Any non-compete clauses or restrictions?" he asked.

"None whatsoever," I replied. "I actually quit six months ago after the incident."

He looked relieved. "We're letting her go. Would you stay on and work directly with us?"

Knowing that DT would handle this properly, I simply said "Yes," knowing this was another pivotal moment in my journey. (I'm still with DEF CON today, doing my part to guide these events through more than two decades of growth.)

But the story doesn't end there. Over the next couple of years, she occasionally called me for help with events. I maintained professional courtesy but kept firm boundaries.

Then came the strangest request of all. "I really feel bad about things," she told me over lunch at an upscale restaurant she'd insisted on. "I want to make it up to you. How about going to England for a week? I'll cover everything."

Initially, it seemed generous, but her insistence on specific dates grew increasingly suspicious. She became agitated when I suggested alternatives.

Finally, I confronted her: "What's really going on here? This doesn't feel right."

After much hedging, the truth emerged. She had been pursuing one of our married clients—a charming British executive—and learned his wife would be away, leaving him with their young children. When she suggested a weekend getaway, he declined because he had no childcare. Her "generous" offer to send me to England was actually so I could babysit his children—his wife's knowledge— while she seduced him at a nearby hotel.

"I'm not doing that," I told her firmly. "You're trying to manipulate me into helping you manipulate him and potentially destroy his family."

Her response was defensive: "It's just a bit of fun—nobody would be hurt. I've already booked some of it, so you really need to make this work."

I didn't go to England, and we never spoke again. It was the final confirmation that my earlier decisions had been correct.

Looking back across the decades, I see how these decisive moments shaped not just my career but my understanding of professional ethics. By refusing to be manipulated or intimidated, I discovered a path that aligned with my values while leveraging my unique skills.

What began as a challenging relationship with a toxic colleague ultimately led me to a community that has sustained me for over twenty-five years. The tech conference world became my unexpected home—a place where my film production background, event management skills, ethical boundaries, and bringing Shamanic tools and understanding created a foundation for lasting success.

Sometimes our most significant growth springs from our firmest "no." Sometimes, the universe guides us to exactly where we belong, disguised as a series of obstacles. And sometimes, standing your ground leads you to discover you've been standing in exactly the right place all along.

Ciara Lewis

Owner of KLConsulting LLC

https://www.linkedin.com/in/ciara-l-51bbbb204/
https://www.facebook.com/KLConsultingLLC/
https://www.instagram.com/klconsultingllc
https://celsjourneys.godaddysites.com

Ciara Lewis, born and raised in Kentucky, started writing poetry at the12. She won her first poetry award in Middle School for an original poem she wrote for her grandma, "Watching Over Me." This was just the beginning of her journey in poetry. Ciara has a background in Medical Information Technology and Medical Billing/Coding. Ciara is the owner of KLConsulting LLC, a Medical Billing and Credentialing Business. Although her background is in Medical Billing, Ciara has always loved helping people through her poetry. Ciara will not only produce poetry books but will in the near future put poetry on blankets, mugs, and more. She is going to be a guiding light for those who are interested in growing as a poet. Connect with Ciara via email at cecespoetrycorner@gmail.com.

Niceness Wins Everytime

By Ciara Lewis

Nice is often defined as pleasant; agreeable; satisfactory. The word itself has a nice ring to it and is straightforward. However, many individuals misinterpret the significance of this word for its true worth and under evaluate it. Some people may even take advantage of this word when it seems fit, leaving those of us who truly value the word to go through some battles and trials. The term "nice" has a much more powerful meaning, especially regarding women. A Nice Girl comes with strength, endurance, patience, obedience, FAITH, encouragement, and most of all, triumphs and setbacks. However, the beauty of a Nice Girl is we don't just WIN, we Finish First.

My whole life, one of my core values was being "nice." My grandmother and mother always told me: "You catch more flies with honey than vinegar." During my school years, I didn't just hang out with one group of people, I hung out with almost everyone. I didn't choose one group because one didn't like the other; I shared my time with all my peers. My mom always said, "Don't put all your eggs in one basket." It's funny because it took me years to fully grasp the importance of the phrase. Now, I realize that if you put all your eggs in one basket and you damage your basket, you will have nothing. It's better to have a variety of people in your circle than the same type of people. It goes along with opposites attract, you may not always see eye to eye with them as you would someone who more matches yourself, but in some weird way, you make things work perfectly. When you listen to music, you don't always hear one instrument, you hear several. That's how you get the true beauty of harmony. I've always been the type of person who wants to help people, I was always looking for ways to help. Throughout high school, many of my friends came to me for guidance, whether it was for advice or just to listen. We never truly know what someone is dealing with behind closed doors, even if we think we do or have some idea. It seems I always attract people who need help or want someone to listen to them. Throughout my professional career, I have often encountered random people who always felt like sharing their life stories or were having some sort of issue and looking for guidance. I would strive to go above and beyond to provide thoughtful advice and support. My niceness paid off for the most part in school, but occasionally it came with a cost. I would find myself in situations where my friends felt neglected, particularly when I helped someone they didn't like or attended events they weren't invited to. I was a sports girl in school, playing soccer and basketball in elementary school and engaging in cheerleading and volleyball throughout middle and high school. When I wasn't playing, I was at either one of the football games or basketball games. As you can imagine, I faced the challenge of balancing these commitments with my friendships. I was either always missing something or late, and although they said they understood, it truly hurt their feelings. Especially because I spent most of my time with people on my teams, and then vice versa when the sports season was over, I would try to shift more of my time to my other friends. This finally started to balance out once we reached high school and my friends realized that I was always going to be there for them, no matter who I was hanging out with or what I was doing. I always let them know how important they were to me. I was that friend who was always checking up on them or trying to plan something for us to get together. I truly valued all my friendships.

After high school, I started realizing that niceness was harder to come by in the adult world and that it would be challenging to remain nice at times. I had no clue about the reality I was about to face. I realized in high school that girls had more of a challenge being nice due to being too competitive. In high school, it was who was the prettiest, after high school, it moved into who went to the best college, who had the best job, who got married and started a family first. It seemed like it was always a race to see who was at the top instead of helping each other reach the top. My first challenge of truly testing my niceness came when I found out I was pregnant with my daughter in my senior year. I had a lot of questions about whether I was pregnant or dropping out of school. However, I received more support rather than judgment, and that came as a shock. This came as a testament to my character, that I had built relationships based on mutual respect and kindness. I never singled people out. I had several friends and teachers reach out to me with love and support. I found out who was truly in my corner at that time. After giving birth to my daughter, I encountered a major health issue, and that is where the real challenge set in. The doctors had left a piece of metal inside of me after delivery that had later caused me to have part of my colon and bowel removed. This caused me to have long-term issues that I still deal with today. It's difficult to be nice when you're constantly in pain, missing out on things, running late, continually going to the doctor, never getting any answers or relief, and trying to raise a child. I knew that acting out of character wouldn't get me very far, so I had to learn to bite my tongue at times, even when I was in severe pain or truly irritated, which was most days. Every time I went to the doctor, they would always compliment me on how strong I was and always in good spirits. I never came in with a nasty attitude, no matter what tests were being done, what medicine I had to take, or how long I would have to wait. They would always tell me I was one of their best patients and they didn't know how I did it. The truth is, it takes a lot to be nice, in my opinion. It takes courage, being knocked down, defeated, growing, understanding, seeing through people and not just for what they seem, in passion and mostly love, lots of love. I believe if you are capable of loving or showing compassion, you are capable of being nice. I believe you must reach down inside and find the ability to be nice, because at the end of the day, and depending on the situation, we all have that choice of being nice or mean. The fact that it's a choice is what makes it even more beautiful and genuine.

After facing significant health challenges, my next challenge came in the form of abuse. My abuser was someone whom I thought I could trust and who cared about me, but I learned very quickly you can't trust everyone. This man spun me directly into his spider web and really did a number on me. I had never seen it coming, because he was one of the nicest people I knew when I first met him, and then one day he became my worst nightmare. I changed for the longest, resulting in me shutting my friends out because of shame and hurt, isolating myself, and allowing bitterness, anger, confusion, and a sense of being lost to take control. The unfortunate thing is, I ended up turning all of that pain and hurt into profanity, and it became my crutch for helping me release the pain and feel better. At least that's what I thought at the time, until years later, I realized it was only hurting me more, not helping me, and it was ugly. It only solved the problem in that one second, but it did not change or improve anything. It most definitely wasn't bettering me as a person. Through all that, I still managed to put on a smile and still be there for others. It wasn't easy; I knew that taking my pain out on those around me wouldn't change the past or undo the harm that had been inflicted. I still struggle to this day, because I truly think someone who has been abused will never 100% get over it. The days may get easier, and thoughts and memories might become less, but there will always be those small things that send triggers to you or reminders. Through my journey, I have learned to manage the aftermath with the support of my therapist, though challenges still arise, sometimes it still gets rough even years later. Writing poetry, journaling, engaging in adult coloring, finding serenity in silence or music, and remaining rooted in prayer have been invaluable tools for me. Some of these tools are also what help me stay true to myself and remain nice.

After facing numerous trials and tribulations, I successfully started my company, KLConsulting LLC, where I assist Medical and Behavioral Health Providers with their billing, credentialing, certain practice setup features, and more. Achieving this goal has allowed me to help others and contribute positively to their professional journeys. I really enjoy what I do and have a very close relationship with all of my providers. My providers/clients chose me because I have managed to maintain my kindness throughout my challenges, as well as my loyalty. I also keep in touch with some of my high school friends. I've learned that kindness can take you far in life if it's a true part of your character. I've always left my previous jobs on good terms and have received several reference letters from most of my former employers. It truly pays to be nice and loyal, because it can take you places in life. Importantly, I didn't compete to reach the top; I achieved success by being kind, treating people with respect, surrounding myself with other women who share similar values and goals, and staying true to who I am.

Becky Mosbrucker

Founder and CEO of Forward Safety Training

https://linkedin.com/in/becky-mosbrucker-9036391a8/
https://www.facebook.com/becky.mosbrucker
https://instagram.com/beckymosbrucker
https://forwardsafetytraining.com
https://beckymosbrucker.com

Becky Mosbrucker is a passionate advocate for women's safety and empowerment. Recognizing the lack of local self-protection training for women in Virginia, she traveled nationwide to learn from top experts before founding her own safety company in 2018. She offers specialized classes in mindfulness, self-protection, and firearm safety, drawing from over two decades of teaching experience. In 2022, she expanded her reach through a safety awareness blog and YouTube channel, leading to collaborations on books, articles, and media appearances. She has contributed to four anthologies, with a fifth set for release in 2025. Beyond personal safety, Becky works with businesses to implement proactive security measures. She is also a board member of the York County Chamber of Commerce and an active community volunteer. Her work continues to inspire confidence and empowerment in others.

She Wins in Business!

By Becky Mosbrucker

It was 2018, and it was not something I ever thought about before. My life had always followed a predictable rhythm, like the steady tick of a clock—unassuming, safe, and anchored in routine. But then, everything shifted. In a very short time, a turn I hadn't seen coming forced me to confront a reality I was not prepared for.

I was trying to break a mold that had been set for years in a culture where I didn't normally fit in. Was it tough? Yes. Did I succeed? Yes. Was it easy? No.

I was working in an area where I was helping others learn a new skill and felt like someone was trying to set me up. The kind of setup that strips you of control, that leaves you grasping at the edges of what you thought you knew. When you're placed in that kind of situation, there's no time to second-guess, no time for hesitation. You have to learn how to pivot very quickly—before it all crumbles beneath you—and pivot is exactly what I did.

When you want something bad enough, you will find a way to get it. It's an undeniable truth, one that keeps you moving forward when all logic screams at you to stop. For me, it was no different. I was brave enough to find out what the requirements were to become an instructor with a local organization, to carve out a space for myself in an industry I admired and one in which I was the minority.

I thought I had it all figured out. I got the business license, the insurance, the training—everything I needed to become "one of them." I imagined myself walking into that classroom with confidence, ready to share my knowledge, ready to help people. But what I received was something completely different.

I had taught safety classes for over 30 years. Working with this particular group was something I really wanted to try. The dream I had so carefully constructed began to unravel the moment I stepped into that first class. I was the minority. I thought I had all the knowledge necessary to teach this topic. I had been working with a company, tasked with instructing students in safety practices. It was early in my safety career, still new, still eager to train students on topics that could save their lives. What I thought I knew about teaching, about running a class, was quickly challenged. The plan I had—an organized, seamless teaching experience—fell apart in front of my eyes. I learned, quickly, that my focus had to shift. No longer was I just thinking about the students in that classroom; no longer was I the teacher I had envisioned. Now, I was the one who needed saving.

I wasn't given the right materials to teach, my presentation had been revised (without my knowledge), and the students did not have a confident way in which to learn. It started small, but over the next few months, it seemed to worsen. The materials I was given were damaged, and I was expected to demonstrate how they worked correctly, in a class of approximately 20 students.

Then, there was the method I was told to follow—a rigid, one-size-fits-all approach that didn't work for everyone. It was nothing like what I had been used to and not the way I had been trained or envisioned connecting with my students.

It was loud, noisy, chaotic—and yet somehow, they thought that was the way you were supposed to instruct a class of students. I certainly wasn't used to that and didn't understand how a student could learn in that environment.

Then came the final blow—the last straw that broke whatever hope I had left. A presentation had been revised, but I only found out about it when I was at the front of the classroom, ready to teach it. I was expected to present material that I hadn't seen, let alone had time to prepare for. The anxiety hit me hard. The whole situation felt like a setup—like the rug was being pulled out from under me at every turn.

To say I felt bullied would have been an understatement. But the truth, deep down, was that I wasn't just being bullied. I was being broken down. Piece by piece, they chipped away at my confidence, at my passion, until I was nothing but a shell of the person who had walked into that room, full of ambition and hope.

At first, I internalized everything. I convinced myself that maybe I wasn't good enough, that I didn't belong there. I questioned my skills, my worth, and my ability to succeed. But then, something inside me snapped. I realized that I wasn't the problem—the environment was. The people around me weren't trying to uplift or support me; they were trying to tear me down. And I refused to let them succeed.

I will admit, today, some years later, I would have done things differently. I would have stood up for myself, demanded explanations for their actions, and refused to accept the chaos and disorganization. But back then, in the thick of it all, I cowered. I hid my head between my legs and buried myself in embarrassment. I thought that maybe, just maybe, if I stayed quiet, it would all blow over and I would forget about it.

What this experience did do for me, however, was to ignite a passion within me to start my own business. Since I had already obtained the necessary credentials—a license, insurance, and training—I was fully equipped to establish my own company and teach in a way that truly resonated with me.

Starting a business had never been on my radar. I had always worked for others, never once considering the possibility of forging my own path. But after what I had just endured, I knew one thing for certain: I never wanted to go through that again. By becoming my own boss, I could ensure that I would never be treated that way again, nor would I allow any of my employees to experience this same kind of treatment.

I built my business on a foundation of respect, integrity, and a commitment to high-quality education. I created an environment where instructors were supported, where students felt encouraged, and where learning was engaging and effective.

My goal is to teach in a way that prioritizes my students' well-being. I have always been empathetic, but now more than ever, I strive to create an environment where every student feels safe, valued, and heard. I want them to feel comfortable asking questions and confident that I will respond with patience and understanding. Learning is not one-size-fits-all, and as an instructor, it is my responsibility to adapt my teaching methods to accommodate different learning styles.

What do my students say about my training? They leave with a clear understanding of the subject matter. They gain a newfound appreciation for the topic. Most importantly, they walk away feeling confident and self-assured in their knowledge and abilities.

Today, I stand not as a victim of bullying but as a survivor who transformed adversity into opportunity. I turned my pain into a purpose, using my experiences to fuel a business that stands for everything I once lacked: fairness, preparation, and unwavering support. And for that, I am grateful.

At Forward Safety Training, I try to make sure my students gain the knowledge they once were seeking, making them feel safe and valued.

What can you do next? Attend one of my classes and see what my other students are saying. I have in-person and online classes. I teach Situational Awareness classes, college girl safety, middle school girl safety, single women safety, and older women safety—as you can see, I am all about keeping our ladies safe! I also have a few classes for men. My goal is to help educate the world with a safety mindset so they will not be someone's next victim.

Please reach out to me for more information - forwardsafetytraining@gmail.com

Thank you and stay safe.

Becky Mosbrucker

Owner, Forward Safety Training, LLC

Megan Dirks

Brandosaurus Meg
Brand Coach

https://www.linkedin.com/in/megannovas/
https://www.facebook.com/brandosaurusmeg
https://www.instagram.com/brandosaurusmeg
https://www.brandosaurusmeg.com/
https://www.thegirlontheleft.com/

Megan Dirks is a serial entrepreneur, certified professional coach, and the creator of The Girl on the Left project. Collaborating with 20+ inspiring women, Megan brings raw, transformative stories to life, flipping the script on traditional before-and-after narratives. She celebrates the mess and the milestones of growth, encouraging readers to honor every chapter of their lives. Operating as Brandosaurus Meg is her primary business, she helps solopreneur coaches build bold, confident, and unforgettable brands that stand out. With over a decade of experience in marketing, wellness, and business strategy, Megan blends mindset coaching with design expertise to craft authentic, impactful identities. Inspired by storytelling, animals, and gaming, she embraces growth and rejects harmful vices, believing every venture is an adventure, and a chance to add lasting good to the world. Megan travels full-time as a nomadic pet-sitter, creating stories, brands, and projects that connect and inspire.

Nice Girls Finish First: Protect Your Peace, Without Losing Your Heart

By Megan Dirks

Calling myself "nice" isn't the first thing that comes to mind, not because I think I'm mean, but because it's a label that comes with many expectations, especially for women in business.

I'm thoughtful, I think before I speak, and am generous with my time and energy. These traits shape how others view me, both professionally and personally.

Here's the twist: when you're consistently kind and giving, people start expecting it, like it's a rule rather than a choice. Set a boundary, and suddenly you're not "nice" anymore. You're seen as difficult or unkind when you're really just being clear about what you can handle.

I'm here to help heart-centered entrepreneurs strike the balance between kindness and standing firm in business. By finding this balance, you can avoid burnout, resentment, and losing sight of who you are in the process.

Remember, the most important person to be kind to is yourself, because true kindness begins with self-respect.

My phone is always filled with growth and personal development content, and that's just the world I live in. Even without big programs, you pick up things along the way from bite-sized content. Powerful women in these spaces often share reminders that hit at just the right time.

Brené Brown's got it right: true kindness isn't about people-pleasing, it's about being clear and direct. Setting boundaries doesn't make you mean; it makes you honest. That hit me hard when I learned that people with the strongest boundaries are the most compassionate because they don't build up resentment from over-giving.

In *Dare to Lead*, she drops this truth bomb: avoiding tough conversations to "be nice" only breeds resentment and dysfunction. "Clear is kind. Unclear is unkind." Mic drop.

Mel Robbins nails it too in *The Five Second Rule*: "Saying yes to things you don't want to do is a form of self-betrayal." It's tough, but saying no with confidence without over-explaining is key.

In my early thirties, I've learned that being nice doesn't mean saying "yes" to everything. Sometimes, saying "no" *is* the kindest thing you can do for both yourself and others. It's tricky to navigate, especially with our people-pleasing instincts, but the people who truly respect your kindness will value your time, energy, and expertise. They won't just see you as a resource.

Let's talk about what I call the Generosity Tax. Women, especially in coaching, service-based businesses, and self-development spaces, are often expected to give more for less, whether that's free advice, discounted work, or emotional labor. Not cool!

That pressure to constantly be super-duper helpful can lead to burnout and resentment. The kicker is that when you finally stop, some people act like you've changed for the worse or even treat you like a villain.

We need to reframe the narrative of being nice versus being fair. You can be kind while still charging what you're worth and protecting your energy. Instead of reactive generosity like offering endless discounts or free work out of guilt, you can create structure and limits around your pro-bono adventures.

Yeah, I used to do that too, until I was fried and done.

In my early twenties, I found myself working with small business owners who just didn't get how powerful branding really is. I'd meet people with websites that looked like they hadn't been touched in a decade, logos that didn't make a statement, and a brand story? Nonexistent. There was this one local hotel I remember—super popular, always fully booked. But their website? A mess. No professional email, no online booking system (hello?!). Honestly? It just felt sketchy to anyone who wasn't a local.

So, I got the bright idea to pitch them a whole new vision: a modernized brand that would make them shine. I spent hours creating polished mockups, clear plans, and a vision that could really help them grow. But when I presented it? All I got was a shrug and a "If it ain't broke, don't fix it."

Ouch. That was frustrating. I had given so much time and energy to something that clearly didn't matter to them. But here's the thing I learned: just because you give doesn't mean others will see the value in what you're offering. Sometimes, it's a tough pill to swallow, but we don't have to let those moments define us.

Lesson Learned: I stopped wasting energy trying to convince people that their business deserves better branding if they don't see it themselves. I realized it's more important to work with clients who value my time and are ready to evolve.

You can absolutely be yourself, be kind, and set expectations from the get-go. Don't let people challenge those boundaries. Choose generosity wisely and give value where it truly matters, not where it just eats up your time.

Nice girls do finish first... when they do it the smart way. Being kind, generous, and approachable builds trust and creates strong relationships, both in business and in life.

When you make people feel valued, they're more likely to recommend you and come back for more. A reputation for kindness can open doors that pure skill or strategy might not.

You can teach technical skills, but human values and soft skills? Not so much. If I were building a team, I'd hire based on character first and invest in teaching the rest, no question.

When I started building my web design and branding coaching portfolio, I'd approach local small businesses and entrepreneurs who clearly didn't enjoy handling their own marketing. I'd offer my services for free, and even now, when I come across someone I truly believe in, I can't help but offer to help them shine up their brand.

I don't always get paid for these, but I'm proud to say that for over five years, word of mouth kept me fully booked. It even helped me maintain a waitlist when I wasn't feeling up to in-person networking or other marketing adventures.

I'm a bit of a hermit and tend to get drained easily in social situations, so avoiding endless sales calls and the social media circus was a game-changer. It was amazing waking up to DMs from strangers wanting to hire me immediately.

While I don't want to rely on that and get lazy in other areas of my business, the reputation I earned really allowed me to breathe in periods of life that I was a little more crunched. It's also made me insanely grateful for the genuine, long-term client loyalty I've earned, too. Many clients have been with me for over two years, and I feel incredibly honored by that.

It's also my personal belief that being nice is a competitive advantage when paired with confidence and boundaries. The best business leaders and mentors I've met are both compassionate and firm. The key is to be *nice and respected*, not *nice and taken for granted*.

One of the hardest lessons I learned was working with peers who crossed the line into "friend" territory. What started as a discounted gig and skill swap turned into a full-blown nightmare of scope creep and unmet expectations. A simple project turned into a time-sucking monster.

When they asked for some new inclusions, I did something I'd never done before: I sent a follow-up invoice for the additional hours. Their reaction? Shock. Offense. They were upset I'd charge for work we had clearly agreed was new.

The project dragged on for *months*, and I found myself drowning in unpaid hours, troubleshooting, and dealing with their entitled attitude. It was a wake-up call to either keep giving away my time for free or stand up for myself and get it done.

Lesson Learned: Never let familiarity blur professionalism. Even with the best intentions, people can unknowingly take advantage. It's up to you to set boundaries and own your worth.

These types of projects seem to pop up every year or two, just to challenge me. It's like the universe is testing me to see if I'll slip back into old patterns or if I'll stick to what I've learned. Now, I lovingly call them "reminders." These "reminder" projects have helped me fine-tune my boundaries and build resilience. Every time one pops up, I handle it with more grace and more firmness.

With more clarity and self-awareness, I can spot these moments coming a mile away. I see the signs, and I know when it's time to either set a stronger boundary or walk away.

In doing so, I've cut out risking resentment and burnout, letting me feel aligned, feminine, and well, *nice* while operating my business.

Now, it's your turn.

If you've felt this way, take a step back and reflect for clarity. Identify where you're over-giving and practice saying no without long-winded explanations.

Take a moment to identify where you're over-giving and practice saying "no" without guilt. Being nice isn't about giving endlessly, it's about being intentional and assertive. Setting boundaries is a form of self-respect and a way to make space for what truly matters.

Start today, and watch how protecting your time and energy leads to more niceness, confidence, and growth. You'll flourish at home and in business.

Sonia Rodrigues

Transition to Wellness
Psychotherapist & Life Transition Coach

https://www.linkedin.com/in/sonia-rodrigues-48b87149/
https://www.facebook.com/SoniaRodriguesLPC/
https://instagram.com/transition.to.wellness
https://www.transitiontowellness.com/
https://soniarodrigues-marto.tribesites.com

Sonia Rodrigues has been a licensed psychotherapist for over 20 years. She is the owner of a psychotherapy and coaching practice called Transition to Wellness. She has worked with people of all ages, helping them navigate various challenges in their life. She utilizes a holistic approach and provides a safe and supportive environment where her clients can feel supported on their path towards healing from their traumatic experiences and guided towards creating the life they desire. She provides individual therapy, coaching and also offers a variety of workshops on topics related to trauma, post-traumatic growth and fostering resilience.

Rising Above: The Transformative Power of Compassion

By Sonia Rodrigues

The Role of Compassion in Rising Above Our Struggles

Life rarely unfolds the way we imagine it will. The path to our dreams is almost never linear—it twists and turns, taking us through valleys of heartache, unexpected detours, disappointments, and lessons we never anticipated. At times, it can feel like everything is falling apart just when we thought we were getting closer to where we wanted to be. Yet it is through these very challenges that we are invited to rise above and that often propel us into something greater.

These hardships aren't detours from our path—they are the path. They shape us, stretch us, and prepare us for what's next in ways comfort never could. They call us to pause, to feel, to process—not to bypass the pain or rush into the next distraction, but to sit with it, to learn from it, and to allow it to teach us something essential about who we are and who we are becoming. When we choose not to numb or ignore our struggle, we open ourselves to deeper resilience, wisdom, and empathy. We begin to see growth when we stop and examine what our struggles are teaching us and how they are making us stronger.

It is important to recognize that while we each carry our own burdens—stress, loss, self-doubt, or disappointment—others are often carrying invisible burdens of their own. That sharp tone in an email, the unexpected criticism, or someone's emotional distance may not be a reflection of us at all, but rather a glimpse into their own inner struggles. Compassion invites us to see beyond the surface, to consider that pain often wears many disguises. It empowers us to pause before reacting, to take a breath instead of taking offense, and to choose understanding over assumption. In doing so, we reclaim our emotional power—we respond not from a place of wounded pride, but from grounded wisdom and grace. Compassion does not excuse harmful behavior, but it gives us perspective—and in that perspective lies freedom. Compassion gives us the power to pause before reacting, to choose grace over retaliation, and to respond from a place of wisdom rather than woundedness.

When we look at the world through compassionate eyes, we stop internalizing everything as a personal failure or attack. Instead, we begin to understand the interconnectedness of our human experience. We begin to heal, not because our challenges vanish, but because our perspective changes. We stop striving to "win" in the traditional sense and begin to define success as peace, empathy, and personal growth.

How Compassion Can Be a Catalyst for Healing and Empowering Others

Compassion has the extraordinary power to mend what the world often overlooks. In a society that frequently rewards performance over presence, achievement over authenticity, and speed over stillness, compassion invites us to slow down and *see* one another— truly see. When we meet someone in their pain without trying to fix or judge them, we create a sacred space for healing. In that space, shame begins to loosen its grip, and self-worth begins to take root. Compassion says, "You are not broken. You are human. And you are not alone." And in that moment, healing begins—not just for the one receiving it, but for the one giving it too. But compassion doesn't stop at comfort—it lifts us up. It reminds others of their strength when they've forgotten. It empowers them to believe in themselves again. One kind word, one act of grace, one moment of presence can be the catalyst that transforms despair into courage, doubt into confidence, and isolation into connection. Compassion is not just a feeling—it's a force. And when we lead with it, we help others rise, not because we have all the answers, but because we remind them that they already hold everything they need inside.

What makes compassion so powerful is that it creates a ripple effect. When someone experiences true compassion, it awakens something within them—a sense of safety, belonging, and possibility. They begin to see that vulnerability is not weakness, but a doorway to deeper connection and strength. And often, those who have been shown compassion become the ones who extend it to others. That is how healing multiplies. That's how communities, families, and workplaces are transformed—from the inside out. In showing up with open hearts, we begin to rewrite the silent scripts so many of us have carried: that we have to earn love, prove our worth, or carry our pain alone. Compassion replaces those lies with truth: *You are enough. You are worthy of kindness. You deserve to be seen and supported just as you are.* When we embody this truth and extend it freely, we don't just empower others—we give them permission to reclaim their voice, their courage, and their light while recognizing their self-worth. That is the quiet, beautiful transformation compassion creates—one heart at a time.

The Transformative Effect of Compassionate Leadership

Leadership that changes lives doesn't bark orders or demand allegiance. It uplifts, listens, and leads by example. A compassionate leader doesn't shy away from accountability, but she enforces it with understanding, not humiliation. She doesn't ignore conflict; instead, she addresses it with curiosity and care.

When a woman leads with compassion, she creates a culture where others feel safe being themselves. In workplaces, this looks like psychological safety—a space where innovation thrives, collaboration deepens, and people take risks not because they have to, but because they feel supported enough to.

Compassionate leadership also means modeling vulnerability. It means saying, "I don't have all the answers," or "That must have been hard," or "Let's work through this together." These are not signs of weakness. They are markers of emotional courage and intelligence.

The ripple effect is profound. Teams led by compassionate leaders tend to outperform those led by fear. Families led with empathy raise children who are more confident and emotionally resilient. Communities that value compassion foster deeper connection and a sense of belonging.

The most transformative leaders aren't the loudest in the room. They are the ones who lead with a calm strength—the kind that comes from knowing that kindness is not a liability; it's a legacy.

Conclusion: How Nice Girls Finish First—And Stay Ahead

For too long, the narrative around kindness—especially in women—has been misrepresented. We've been told that being *nice* is to be naive, being compassionate is to be taken advantage of, and leading with empathy is to lack the grit needed to succeed. But that couldn't be further from the truth.

In reality, compassion is one of the most powerful tools a woman can possess. It fuels resilience, fosters connection, and lays the foundation for meaningful influence in every area of life.

Nice girls finish first not because they are trying to outpace others, but because they are playing an entirely different game—one rooted in purpose, authenticity, and emotional intelligence. They're not driven by ego or competition, but by impact. And because of this, they build something far more enduring than momentary success: they build a legacy.

In business, compassionate women create loyal partnerships, attract value-aligned clients, and lead teams that thrive on trust. They turn coworkers into collaborators and transform pressure into possibility. Their emotional awareness becomes their strategic advantage.

In their careers, nice girls rise not because they demand to be seen, but because their integrity, their consistency, and their care cannot be ignored. They are remembered long after the meeting ends. They build bridges, not silos. And they are often the quiet forces behind the most lasting progress.

In family life, compassion becomes the glue that holds generations together. These women break cycles of silence, nurture emotionally intelligent children, and model what it means to love without conditions but with clear boundaries. They create homes where everyone can breathe a little easier.

And in their personal lives, compassionate women build circles of depth, not just breadth. Their friendships are soul-deep. Their romantic relationships are based on mutual respect and vulnerability. They don't just surround themselves with people—they create *belonging*.

Compassion doesn't mean saying yes to everything or tolerating mistreatment. Quite the opposite—it's the strength to say, "I care deeply, and I also know my worth." Compassionate women are not doormats—they are doors to transformation, for themselves and for others.

So when we say "nice girls finish first," we're not talking about the outdated image of politeness that silences truth or plays small to be liked. We're talking about the woman who leads with open-hearted strength. The one who holds space and sets boundaries. The one who knows that real power doesn't come from domination, but from deep connection, trust, and authenticity.

She wins—not because she conforms, but because she *cares*, and still dares to rise. She wins because people believe in her. Because she uplifts others and, in doing so, elevates herself. Because her kindness is not performative—it's transformative.

So, here's to the compassionate women. The nice girls. The boundary-setters. The quiet warriors. The gentle revolutionaries.

You are not just finishing first—you are changing the game entirely.

Ada Cook

https://linktr.ee/adacook

Ada Cook is the CEO of Fear Kickers Corporation and Founder of the Fear Kickers Community, where she empowers individuals to transform their body, mind, and finances. Recognized by Global Women of Choice 2024 and serving as an ambassador for both LIGHT beamers and Mindset Mastery 360, Ada is passionate about helping others break through fear and unlock their greatest potential. By sharing parts of her own journey, she hopes to impact and inspire people to bounce back from adversity and create a life of purpose and fulfillment. A dynamic individual, Ada is an army wife, dog mom, digital marketing expert, health and finance coach, artist, pianist, and photographer. Born and raised in Hong Kong, she moved to the U.S. in 2014 and now resides in New Braunfels, Texas, with her husband, Brandon, where they enjoy their life together and support each other's dreams.

Be Kind to You

By Ada Cook

Growing up in a Chinese traditional family, kindness wasn't exactly the lesson we were taught, at least not in the way I needed it. We were expected to be strong, resilient, and hardworking. Self-sacrifice was noble, and self-criticism was a sign of humility. I don't blame my family. They raised me the way they knew best, shaped by their own hardships and survival instincts, but somewhere along the way, I learned that being kind to myself wasn't a priority. It wasn't even an option.

I remember my family constantly reminding me to push harder, to do better, to never let myself become weak. If I cried over a mistake, I was told to wipe my tears and move on. If I was struggling, I was reminded that others had it worse. If I dared to feel proud of something I had achieved, I was told that I was bragging too much. In our culture, there was always an expectation to be strong and endure. I never learned how to be gentle with myself in that process.

For years, I internalized the belief that kindness was something you gave to others, not something you extended to yourself. I thought being hard on myself would make me better, so I pushed through exhaustion, berated myself for my imperfections, and constantly told myself I wasn't enough. I carried that mindset into my teenage years, adulthood, my marriage, my work—into everything. It became second nature.

Until life taught me I couldn't live like this forever.

As a teenager, the mirror was my enemy. Acne became my worst nightmare. Not just a few breakouts here and there, but severe, soul-crushing acne that covered my face, forehead, and chin. It completely stole my confidence. I couldn't bear to look in the mirror, let alone have my photo taken. I convinced myself that my worth was tied to my appearance, and since my skin was "flawed," I was unworthy of being seen.

No one in my family really talked about self-esteem. The response was mostly practical: *"Drink more water." "Don't eat fried food." "Just wash your face more."* No one told me, *"Hey, you're beautiful no matter what."* I spoke to myself in the worst way possible. I called myself ugly, worthless. I avoided eye contact with people. I spent years hiding; I hated how I looked.

Acne wasn't the only thing that made me feel different. I was born with multiple hereditary exostoses (MHE), a genetic disorder that causes benign bone tumors to grow along my limbs. While others had smooth, straight legs and toes, I had bones that jutted out in places they weren't supposed to. My right thigh had a large visible bone sticking out, and my toes weren't aligned like everyone else's. I remember looking at them and feeling defective, like my body had betrayed me.

I would sit and stare at my leg, wondering why I couldn't just be "normal." Why did my body have to be different? I avoided sandals because I didn't want people staring at my toes. I was hyper-aware of the way my pants fit over my leg, hoping no one would notice the abnormality. I refused to wear shorts and skirts. Once again, instead of being kind to myself, I let the shame settle in. I told myself my body wasn't beautiful, that I wasn't enough because I didn't look like everyone else.

Eventually, I had surgery to remove two significant bone tumors. The physical pain was one thing, but the emotional scars took much longer to heal. Even after the bones were gone, I still carried the years of insecurity with me. Surgery fixed my leg, but it didn't fix how I saw myself. That emotional part of healing took something deeper.

You see, changing the outside doesn't automatically heal what's broken on the inside. I had spent years believing that if I could just fix the things I didn't like about myself—my skin, my body, my outlook—then maybe I'd finally feel enough. I'd look at myself and not feel ashamed. I'd shed the weight of self-criticism I had carried for so long. Yet, when the surgery was over, when the external "problem" was gone, somehow the shame, the self-doubt, and the belief that I wasn't good enough were still there. The scars left behind weren't just on my body; they were etched into the way I spoke to myself, the way I shrank in front of others, and the way I believed I had to earn my worth.

Healing, real healing, wasn't about changing how I looked. It wasn't about erasing the imperfections. It was about unlearning the belief that I had to be flawless to be worthy. It was about undoing years of self-judgment and showing myself the compassion I so easily gave to others.

I deserve kindness simply because I exist. This mindset was the hardest thing to accept. It required me to sit with the parts I hated about myself and had always tried to hide, to face them and show love instead of criticism. That kind of healing doesn't happen until you stop tearing yourself apart and start speaking to yourself with the same kindness that you'd offer to the people you love. That kind of healing isn't about changing who you are but accepting all of who you are.

If there was ever a moment that tested my ability to show myself kindness, it was when I lost my health coaching business. Six years of work, of building a global team, of pouring my heart and soul into something—gone, just like that. I had 30 days to say goodbye to my income, my community, and the identity I had built around it.

At first, I did what I had always done: I blamed myself. I told myself I should have been smarter, that I should have seen it coming, that I had failed. I let the shame of it consume me because, in my mind, failure meant I wasn't enough.

Something inside me cracked. Maybe it was exhaustion. Maybe it was the fact that I had spent years running on empty, always trying to prove something to myself and others. Maybe it was just the quiet whisper of God reminding me that I wasn't defined by what I had lost.

Taking a deep breath, I allowed myself to grieve without guilt. I stopped forcing myself to "just get over it" and instead let myself feel—the frustration, the sadness, the uncertainty, everything. In that space of raw honesty, I realized I had never truly been kind to myself before.

When I look back at my life, that girl who was never taught to love herself, who struggled with severe acne, who hid her body because of bone tumors, who worked tirelessly only to lose everything overnight, who spent years believing she wasn't enough... is now someone who fought her way through, who learned to rewrite her story, who chose, day by day, to be a little kinder to herself. I still have flaws. My skin isn't perfect even after years of healing. My body still carries the marks of MHE. I still battle self-doubt, but I know those things don't define me.

Kindness to myself is something I still work on daily, but I know now that it's not selfish. It is not a weakness. It is the foundation of everything else—my happiness, my relationships, my ability to keep moving forward even when life doesn't go as planned.

More than anything, kindness to myself has set me free.

Free from the weight of never feeling enough. Free from the constant need to prove my worth. Free from the voice in my head that once told me I had to be perfect before I could be proud of myself. I can let go of the endless striving, the impossible expectations, the guilt of not always having it together. I can embrace myself as I am—not as a project to be fixed, but as someone who is already whole.

Self-compassion creates a quiet peace as I stop fighting against myself. I no longer have to run, hide, or shrink myself to fit some unattainable version of who I think I should be. Instead, I can just be me. In that space where grace replaces pressure, I feel free.

So, if you're like me, if you've spent years being too hard on yourself, if you've believed the lie that you have to earn your worth, if you've been waiting for permission to be gentle with yourself... Let this be your permission slip.

You don't have to wait until you've "fixed" everything about you to be kind to yourself. You don't have to wait until you've achieved some impossible standard to believe you are worthy of love.

You are enough now.

You deserve kindness now.

When you start treating yourself with love and compassion, you don't just change your life, you inspire others to do the same.

That, I believe, is the true power of kindness. And it starts with you.

Stephanie Dauble

The Fullest Stories
Luxury Reinvention Strategist | Transformational Storytelling &
High-Performance Branding

https://www.linkedin.com/in/stephaniedauble/
https://www.facebook.com/sdauble
https://www.instagram.com/daubleganger
https://medium.com/@stephanie.dauble

Stephanie Dauble is a bestselling author, visionary leader, and reinvention strategist who turns brokenness into beauty. A former corporate executive, she left the boardroom to build a global brand centered on radical resilience, reinvention, and luxury transformation. Through her writing, storytelling, and immersive experiences, she empowers others to reclaim their narrative, elevate their lives, and rise into audacious greatness. With a unique ability to blend grit and grace, Stephanie dismantles generational limitations and redefines what's possible—proving that reinvention isn't just for the privileged but for anyone bold enough to claim it. Whether guiding high-achievers through their next chapter or crafting cinematic brand stories, she champions a life lived fully, fearlessly, and unapologetically. Her work is a rallying cry for those ready to step into the extraordinary, proving that the glow-up isn't just an aesthetic—it's a way of life.

Untangling the Nice Girl Myth: From Pushover to Powerhouse

By Stephanie Dauble

Introduction: The Moment of Realization

His text took my breath away.

"I'm not in love with you anymore."

After the initial gut-punch moment wore off, I first thought how very *Sex and the City* Jack Berger of him to break off a month-long relationship over text. My second thought was ouch. Not because it was all that painful, but because I had been thinking about ending things too and didn't. It just didn't feel like the "nice" thing to do.

In that moment of reckoning, I found myself deeply reflecting on how many occasions I yearned for a relationship that was less compartmentalized and more full. I wasn't truly happy, either. I've always wanted a love that's all-encompassing and vibrant, not polite to the detriment of growth. Though neither of us seemed thrilled with how it was progressing, we chose to stay together despite it all. Until we didn't.

This personal revelation led me to question the very essence of "niceness" and how it often confines us, especially as women.

The Illusion of Niceness

There's a myth we've been sold—a pretty little lie wrapped in a bow of politeness and self-sacrifice.

The myth is that if we are "nice" enough, agreeable enough, selfless enough, we will be loved. Rewarded. Chosen. That being easygoing and endlessly accommodating will open doors, build relationships, and somehow, miraculously, bring us fulfillment.

But here's what they don't tell you:

Niceness, when it's conditioned rather than chosen, is a leash.

It tethers you to the comfort of others while keeping you miles away from your own power. It whispers that your worth is measured by how much of yourself you are willing to give away. And the result? You become the woman who stays quiet when she should speak. Who apologizes for taking up space. Who shrinks herself to fit into a world that was never designed to hold her in her full force.

That's not power.

That's not kindness.

That's self-abandonment.

And that is exactly how nice girls become pushovers.

The Trap of Performative Niceness

For years, I thought being nice meant being good. That if I just made myself likable enough, flexible enough, accommodating enough, I would be valued. That people would treat me the way I treated them.

But niceness, in its performative form, is a dangerous currency.

When your niceness is rooted in pleasing rather than truth, you spend your life in emotional debt—constantly giving, accommodating, and smoothing things over while secretly hoping that someone, somewhere, will give you permission to finally put yourself first.

But that permission? It never comes.

Because people will take what you offer them. And if you've trained the world to expect you to say yes before you've even considered what you really want? They will never ask if you meant no.

The truth is, niceness alone will not save you. It will not protect you. It will not elevate you. Because nice is passive. It is reactive. It is a habit, not a strategy.

And without boundaries, niceness becomes a liability.

The Roots of Niceness: A Personal Reflection

Growing up in a family burdened by the unrelenting grip of heroin addiction, niceness wasn't just a social expectation—it was a survival mechanism. In the chaos of addiction, being agreeable, accommodating, and unobtrusive became essential strategies to navigate the unpredictable terrain of daily life. This form of niceness served as a shield, a way to maintain a semblance of peace amidst turmoil.

Flipping the script on such deeply ingrained behaviors is no small feat; it's a masterclass in fortitude. When niceness is woven into the fabric of your identity from an early age, unraveling it requires immense courage and resilience.

To truly embrace our destiny, we must undertake the challenging yet liberating work of self-examination and change. This involves acknowledging the origins of our compulsive niceness, understanding its initial purpose, and consciously choosing to adopt behaviors that align with our authentic selves. It's about shifting from a place of automatic compliance to one of deliberate and empowered kindness.

The Shift: From Pushover to Powerhouse

There is a way to be kind without being a doormat. A way to move with grace and generosity without betraying yourself in the process. A way to be respected, not for how much you tolerate, but for how boldly and unapologetically you stand in your own self-worth.

And that shift? It comes when you untangle the myth—when you finally realize that real power is not in how small you can make yourself but in how unapologetically you can stand tall.

Here's what it takes to reclaim your power:

1. Replace Niceness with Kindness (There's a Difference)

Niceness is often about compliance. It's the reflex to say "yes" when you mean "no." It's keeping the peace at your own expense.

Kindness, on the other hand, is active. It is deliberate. It is a choice.

- Niceness bends under pressure. Kindness stands firm.
- Niceness seeks approval. Kindness seeks truth.
- Niceness is about being liked. Kindness is about being respected.

The world needs more kind women, not just nice ones.

2. Break the Addiction to Being Liked

If you live for external validation, you will die by its absence.

And yet, so many of us have been taught that our worth is measured by how likable we are. That being agreeable is the key to belonging. That our job is to make others comfortable, even at the cost of our own comfort.

But here's the thing: People can dislike you, and you will not die.

In fact, standing in your truth—owning your "no," prioritizing your peace, refusing to shrink—will almost certainly make some people uncomfortable. And that's a good thing.

Because power is not about universal approval. It's about self-respect.

3. Be Radically Unavailable for Anything That Diminishes You

There is nothing noble about staying small so others can feel big.

There is nothing powerful about saying "yes" to what drains you just because you're afraid of disappointing someone.

There is nothing wise about playing the role of the "nice girl" when what you really want is to be a powerhouse.

The moment you decide that your time, your energy, and your well-being are non-negotiable, your entire world will shift.

Not everyone will like it. And that's the point.

The Powerhouse Mentality

Powerhouses do not abandon their kindness. They reclaim it.

They are kind, but they do not perform.

They are generous, but they do not give out of guilt.

They are loving, but they do not beg to be loved in return.

And they do not wait for permission to take up space.

So, let's set the record straight:

- Nice girls? They don't actually finish last.
- But pushovers do.
- And the difference between the two? Power.

That's not just how you finish first. That's how you win on your own beautiful terms.

The Final Word: The Power of Self-Sovereignty

When his unceremonious text came through, I didn't rage. I didn't beg. I didn't ask for closure that would never come.

I simply let it be.

Because self-sovereignty is knowing that silence is an answer.

The most powerful response to someone who mistakes your kindness for weakness is no response at all.

That real power isn't loud—it's unshaken.

I didn't need to prove anything. I didn't need to explain why I deserved better. I already knew.

And that's what people misunderstand about the woman who refuses to shrink. They assume she will fight to be heard, when in reality, she is so rooted in her worth that she doesn't need to say a thing.

So, let's set the record straight one last time:

Being nice isn't the goal.

Being kind isn't the problem.

But being unapologetically sovereign in your one and only life?

That's the power move.

Dorothe Philippe

Mentor in Intuition and Telepathy

https://www.linkedin.com/in/dorothephilippe/
https://facebook.com/dorothe.philippe?locale=fr_FR
https://instagram.com/dorothe.philippe/?hl=fr
https://www.dorothephilippe.com

Dorothe Philippe is a mentor in intuition and telepathy with more than twenty years of experience. She is German living in France, mother of four grown up children and a passionate rider since her young age. Her journey started when a healer saved her family from a tragic destiny and taught her to tap into her intuition, an innate capacity we all possess. Dorothe then got chosen by Volcano, a young former stunt horse difficult to approach. Volcano taught her how we may become more conscious of our thoughts, emotions, actions and the language we use, so we may be aligned, succeed and lead a happy life. In addition to her work as a life coach, animal psychologist and healer, Dorothe engages today to share valuable information about our inborn abilities of intuition and telepathy, in order to allow us to know more and expand our true potential.

Knowing Who We Are

By Dorothe Philippe

I was galloping my horse at the other end of the huge outdoor arena when I saw the trainer tapping one of the horses from the stables with a touchier whip impatiently against the hind legs. The trainer was by the horse's foot, and the owner was on its back, and it was obvious that they were trying to teach the horse a new exercise. The horse did not seem to understand what they wanted, which was understandable, as I could see that the aids were not clear and even contradictory. It could also have been that the horse was not able to execute the demanded movements. This actually happens quite often, as a lot of horses suffer from pain, and unfortunately, nobody ever remarks on it. The coach then asked the owner to dismount, and they switched roles. As the horse still refused to execute the asked movement, the coach got upset, took the reins short, and gave the horse several violent blows with the dressage whip while the owner went from behind with the touchier whip. That's when I pulled over to intervene. A row with the trainer exploded, followed by the dead, still silence, arguments generally left in the air. I do not normally have rows. I usually know how to stay calm and find the right words. Arguments make me sad. They may move you or others in the same or a different way. Conflicts are overwhelming for everybody. They remind us painfully how much we are actually lacking in knowledge and tools to handle relationships and remedy situations.

I had finished with my horse and was now on the way back to my car. My mind and heart were still overflowing with emotions when I caught sight of the horses along the arena and those who had witnessed the scene. More than twenty years ago, in one of the darkest moments of my life, I discovered that we all possess the innate faculty of intuition and telepathy and have the capacity to heal. From then on, I have taken the habit of sitting with myself and turning inwards when I need help and guidance. You may tune into your intuition by simple intention. To obtain information, ask logical and intuitive questions and pay attention to what comes up first. I became a certified animal therapist and animal psychologist, a professional animal communicator, a healer, a life coach and mentor in telepathy and intuition, and a co-author. However, I am, above all, a student of life. I observe nature, animals, and anything I find inspiring to learn and understand, so that I may be able to make shifts in myself, set myself free from limiting beliefs, become clear about my real values, and focus on what I really want and desire.

I had opened my car door and wanted to get in. All the horses were looking at me now. Their heads were up, their ears pointed forward, including the one I had advocated for. Instead of getting into my car, I closed the door again, knowing that they looked at me like this to help. Animals feel distress. They are very empathic and peaceful. This is probably why we love them so much and feel so pleasant in their presence. "How do we get over fights and back to what is really important?" I silently asked the horses in my mind. The horses started to radiate love in response.

I do not know if you have ever had the chance to meet a person, an animal, or find yourself in a sacred place vibrating with unconditional love. It is an indescribable feeling. It is so beautiful, soothing, blissful, profound, and different from anything that it is actually not to be put into words. Time stands still. You forget who you are, what you have become, what you have just lived or thought. Your whole being just becomes still. Everything stops. There is only love. There is nothing in you that resists. You just let it happen. You receive and nothing is asked. You become one with love. You are love. And, you do not want it to end.

Coming home, I arranged for a quiet moment to sit and tune back into the horses' energy. Hands on my heart, I tried to get back into the state they had put me. In our relationships, we are usually looking for something in return, we want results or outcomes, we judge, we have our certainties and beliefs, turn around in internal discussions in our minds, and so on. Unconditional, however, means free of anything. Free of thoughts. Free of emotions. Free of expectations. Free of forgiving yourself. Free of forgiving another. Free of doing anything. Just being. Being love and flow. Love to all the beings involved. Love to yourself. Love into the situation. Love into what just happened. Love into the farther past. Love into the present. Love into the future. No matter what the problem is. No matter what the situation is. No matter what gravity is involved. Unconditional love can be your remedy to all. Love allows one to become whole. It is the language of the soul. We all need to become whole again. This is why healers tune into the vibration of love. It is love that is needed most desperately. If you practice this, miracles of all sorts happen.

The day after, the trainer came around the corner with her horse. She did not say hello. I took my courage and stepped in her way. In difficult situations, I try to let go and ask to be guided, so that I may find the right words. I then trust the process. Somehow, we were able to talk. I learned from someone else later that the trainer had been orphaned and gone through a lot of hardship as a child. I was happy to have asked the horses for advice. Animals always know what is needed and what is important in the now. Instead of asking an animal, you may also ask your higher self, or turn to the space around you. There will always be an answer. You will hear, see, or feel it. If you want to send love to a person, an animal, or into a situation, just think of it. Telepathy travels over time and space, and you can send your message from wherever you want. Trust the process. Love, intuition, and telepathy are innate.

My story reflects just a little of what we live daily in our everyday relationships and may be watched all over the world. The term "emotion" arises from the Latin word ex movere, which means going out of the normal state. Emotions may be stored as memory in the body as well as in the electromagnetic field, which is produced by your heart, and which goes several meters beyond your physical body. Uncleared emotions may keep us out of balance for years, engendering physical and psychological difficulties. Certain emotions are even carried on over generations. Identifying emotions is of great help and importance. Clearing emotions has a positive effect on thought and behavior patterns. It also plays an important role in all sorts of healing processes. Tal Schaller is a Swiss doctor of a certain age by now. As a young man, he has worked with indigenous people in the Amazon, and was amazed to state that they are never sick. In wondering what their secret is to their well-being and health, he then observed that they express their emotions systematically. In Western culture, we are taught to do the opposite. We suppress our emotions, push them aside, or ignore them. Emotions, however, are designed to guide and help us. They reveal our inner state. They stand for our truth and are the expression of our higher self. They are drawing our attention to something that has gone away from normal, away from who we really are.

In his book *The Honey Moon Effect*, American cell biologist and founder of Epigenetics Dr. Bruce Lipton reports about the effects of being freshly in love on our life and physiology. We beam, we radiate, we are full of energy, we are inspired and focused, and we feel that everything is possible. We stay open to others, are empathic, and give easily. That's the power of love. Learning to put our emotions into words and to express them in one way or another through grimacing, dancing, running, moving, writing, creating, and doing something that gives us passion, life, and energy helps us to clear our system and to go back to the natural state.

Human psychology states that all beings have the same six basic needs:

- certainty/comfort

- uncertainty/variety
- significance
- love/connection
- growth and contribution

While the first four needs are necessary to survive, the last are more of a spiritual order. Everyone experiences the same six human needs. Each of us has their own way of satisfying those needs and can do it in a positive, neutral, or negative way. Knowing about the six human needs, identifying them in yourself and others, and understanding your own or someone else's patterns and behavior is another great tool to improve relationships and success in life.

May those tools guide and help you. May they support your loved ones, your children and grandchildren, so that they know who they are and be the power of love.

If you want to learn more or need help with an intuitive reading, coaching, mentoring or healing, please feel free to reach out. I am here for you.

Dorothe

https://www.linkedin.com/in/dorothephilippe/
https://facebook.com/dorothe.philippe?locale=fr_FR
https://instagram.com/dorothe.philippe/?hl=fr
https://www.dorothephilippe.com/

Ine-Mari Bredekamp

Ine's Space LLC
Emotional Intelligence Coach and Corporate Trainer

https://www.linkedin.com/in/ine-mari-bredekamp-898a9410b/
https://www.facebook.com/InesSkinSpace
https://www.instagram.com/ine_space
https://nlpinespace.com/
https://inemarispace.com/

Ine-Mari is a leadership trainer, consultant, and freelance violinist based in Dubai. Originally from South Africa, she grew up in a musical family and continues to blend creativity with professional development. As a mother of two teenagers and a widow of an airline pilot, resilience and adaptability have been central to both her personal and professional life. With a strong background in corporate leadership and training, Ine-Mari designs and delivers workshops on emotional intelligence, management skills, and neurodiverse leadership. She is currently studying to become a certified John Maxwell Leadership trainer and is passionate about empowering individuals and organizations. In her free time, she provides ADHD parent training and leads Bible study groups for her church in Dubai. She is also developing the Emotional Resilience

Matrix, a leadership model inspired by Simon Sinek's principles. Through her work, Ine-Mari strives to create meaningful, inclusive, and emotionally intelligent leadership frameworks for diverse professionals.

Emotional Intelligence – Bringing Humanity Back to a World of AI

By Ine-Mari Bredekamp

"You never know how strong you are until
you don't have a choice." – Bob Marley

The world is evolving at an alarming speed. Technology is advancing, artificial intelligence is replacing human jobs, and corporations are prioritizing speed and efficiency over kindness and empathy. In this relentless pursuit of perfection, something essential is being lost. My late husband used to joke that HR no longer stood for "Human Resources" but rather "Human Remains." What was once a lighthearted quip has turned into an unsettling reality. In large corporations, employees are treated as mere statistics, their identities reduced to numbers, their value assessed only in terms of output. Conversations have been replaced with protocols, emotions with efficiency, and human warmth with automated responses. In this hyper-automated world, people are lonelier than ever.

But what happens when life throws a tragedy your way? What happens when you find yourself in desperate need of humanity, only to be met with cold bureaucracy? I faced this exact reality in a country I had called home for over a decade, yet never truly belonged to. My family and I had spent years adapting, integrating, and building a life in a foreign land, knowing deep down that we would never be citizens. We had accepted that reality, but nothing could have prepared us for the way we were treated when tragedy struck.

The expat community is a world of its own—a place where friendships become family, where strangers extend hands in times of need, where support is woven into the very fabric of life. But the corporations that employed us? They were the complete opposite.

When my husband passed away, our expat friends rallied around us, offering warmth and comfort, while the airline he had dedicated years of service to responded with indifference and rigid adherence to policy. It was a shocking contrast that laid bare the absence of human connection in corporate structures.

This is the story of that journey. A story of love, loss, and the pressing need for emotional intelligence in a world that is increasingly driven by artificial intelligence. Because no machine can replace a genuine human connection.

My Journey to Emotional Intelligence Training

My husband and I had a love story that could have been lifted from the pages of a novel. Ours was a whirlwind romance—fast, intense, and deeply real. We met on September 11, 2003, and by the next day, we were already engaged—at least in our hearts. My parents might argue that it was closer to September 24, but for us, the exact date didn't matter. We just knew. A few months later, on February 27, 2004, we were married, ready to face the world together, learning and growing as husband and wife.

He was born to fly. Becoming a pilot wasn't just a career choice; it was his destiny. By thirteen, he was already soaring in gliders, chasing the sky with an insatiable passion. At sixteen, he earned his pilot's license before he even had a driver's license. But beyond his skills as a pilot, he had something else—something rarer. He had emotional intelligence.

He had a remarkable ability to read a room, to make people feel valued, to navigate human emotions with the same precision that he navigated the skies. He had no time for hierarchy or ego—to him, respect was given freely, regardless of rank or title. His colleagues adored him. We only truly grasped the depth of his impact when, after his passing, messages poured in from across the globe. One sentiment stood out among them all: "No matter the destination of your day, it is always a good day when you share the cockpit with Louis."

Yet, despite his natural leadership and emotional intelligence, the corporate world he worked in did not reciprocate his kindness. The toxic leadership culture of the airline weighed on him. For eight years, he remained in the same position, despite being offered direct entry captain when joining, which he politely declined to make sure he learn more about the company before taking the promised advancement. He watched colleagues move forward while he and his group of peers were overlooked, caught in the politics of budget cuts and arbitrary decisions. Eventually, the dream he had worked so hard for was shattered.

He started to lose his drive, his passion, and his joy. And then, he started to lose his health.

When Policies Replace People

My husband had been feeling unwell for some time, but in his airline, taking sick leave was quietly discouraged. It wasn't official, but pilots knew—every sick day could be a black mark on their record. He didn't want to risk it. They were also restricted to the company's private health care at the head office, one which he visited directly after his last flight. They showed him away with the words: "You do not have the position to be able to walk in for help—make an appointment and come back later." He felt humiliated, asking for help and to be shown away, so we waited for him to rest and get better... And we waited too long.

On the day I finally convinced him to go to the hospital, he collapsed at home while I was packing his clothes. In an instant, everything changed.

Even in the aftermath of his passing, the company remained cold and unyielding. I requested a meeting with their HR leadership, hoping to discuss changes to their policies to ensure that no other family would have to endure what we had. When meeting up with the HR, his first words to me were: "Do you not feel that we have supported you enough already?" I thanked him for the support given and asked if I could suggest ways to help their staff never to encounter the lack of support Louis felt when he asked for medical help shortly before his passing. Their response? A short email stating, "Protocols were followed as set by the company, and there will be no further discussion on the matter."

A life had been lost, but to them, he was just a number. A statistic. A case file. And the machine of corporate efficiency moved forward, unbothered.

Disposable Lives in a Digital World

The practical realities of life as a pilot's family meant that when he died, everything tied to his employment disappeared overnight. The house we lived in was company-owned. His contract covered the school fees for our children. Our medical insurance was provided through his job. Within weeks, everything we had built our lives around was stripped away.

I was given six weeks to vacate our home. School fees were cut off without warning. Medical insurance was extended for only a month. Suddenly, during my deepest grief, I was forced to navigate a bureaucratic nightmare, battling red tape, paperwork, and soulless policies.

And then there were the conversations.

I remember trying to close his bank accounts, his phone contract, and his various subscriptions. Time and again, I was met with blank stares, robotic responses, and a lack of understanding. One exchange at a mobile service provider was particularly telling:

Me: "Hi, I need to close my late husband's account. What do I need to do?"

Shop assistant: "You cannot do it for him, ma'am. He needs to come in himself."

Me: "That is not possible. He has passed away."

Shop assistant: "When will he be back?"

Me: "He will not be back. He is dead."

Shop assistant: "I'm sorry, but he needs to close it himself."

The sheer absurdity of it was staggering. But the more I encountered this kind of treatment, the clearer it became: people are no longer trained in empathy. In a world of automation and artificial intelligence, genuine human connection is vanishing.

A New Mission

Louis' death was not in vain. I refused to let it be. That was when I decided to dedicate myself to emotional intelligence training. Leaders, managers, and employees alike need to learn how to communicate, listen, and navigate human emotions. Empathy is not a weakness. Compassion does not slow down productivity. If anything, workplaces that prioritize emotional intelligence thrive. People who feel valued work harder, stay longer, and contribute more.

AI will continue to evolve, replacing tasks that once required human effort. But emotional intelligence? That is the one skill that machines will never master. It is our defining trait. It is what makes us human. And it is time we start prioritizing it again.

Nice girls don't finish last. They finish first. Because in a world starved for kindness, those who lead with emotional intelligence will always be the ones who make the greatest impact. And they will be the ones who bring humanity back to a world that desperately needs it. This girl is crawling but will finish first with an attitude of gratefulness and a mind filled with positivity for our future, showing her kids that Emotional Intelligence is the most important skill you need to advance in the world of leadership.

Author: Ine-Mari Bredekamp (A John Maxwell Leadership Team member)

Shraddha Chandwadkar

Self Esteem & Mindfulness Coach

https://www.linkedin.com/in/shraddhachandwadkar/
https://www.facebook.com/profile.php?id=61558085485911
https://www.instagram.com/luminouslifelabs/
https://shraddhachandwadkar.com/

Shraddha Chandwadkar is a passionate Self-Esteem & Mindfulness coach who empowers women and children. Her workshops, coaching sessions & mini retreats focus on practical strategies to improve confidence, self-image, overcome self-doubt, and develop a positive mindset. They also include mindfulness techniques to increase self-awareness. Shraddha is a published author and has coauthored two bestselling anthologies "Becoming an Unstoppable Woman in Health and Wellness Part 2" and "Pray Don't Panic." She is also a Reiki Master and volunteering as an executive program director in a health and wellness non-profit. She received the 'President Volunteer Service Award' in 2024 acknowledging her service. Shraddha is a mother of two teens and three cats and a spiritual seeker who loves to spend quality time in meditative & contemplative practices. An Engineer by education, Shraddha has an MS, Computer Engineering, from NC State University USA and Bachelors in Electronics Engineering from Pune, India.

Unstoppable Women: The Impact of Female Compassion and Collaboration

By Shraddha Chandwadkar

Women are born nurturers, caregivers, supporters, and healers. Research shows that women who receive unconditional help and support from other women are more likely to succeed in business, attain leadership positions, and drive innovation in various industries.

However, sometimes, we encounter women who want to win by comparison, competition, blaming, criticizing, pushing, and bullying. Does it make them a winner, though?

When we bury our inner strength under the veil of self-doubt, hatred, comparison, and jealousy, we tend to resort to competition, aggression, and bullying. Therefore, every woman must cultivate her inner strength through proper self-care and self-love to be a true winner.

When a woman takes responsibility and empowers herself through self-love, she can understand the pain and needs of other women. Extending kindness to others brings fulfillment in a woman's life and makes her a true WINNER!

Here I am, sharing with you the 7 Qualities for Success that were expressed by women in my life.

7 Qualities for Success

1. Unconditional Love and Support:

My maternal grandmother crossed over to the other side in her sixties. However, her unconditional love, sense of humor, and kindness will remain with me forever. In my childhood years, my father was professionally accomplished but had a challenge with alcoholism. He was on his path to recovery around my mid-teenage years and, with God's grace, family, and friend support, achieved sobriety when I was fifteen. My mother was a schoolteacher then and was very dedicated to her profession. My grandmother used to visit us during my exams to help my mother and support me unconditionally through her loving gestures. It was not that my mother asked for help. However, my grandmother willingly offered to help every single time. While my sister and I studied, she cooked and served us delicious homemade snacks. She was so affectionate that even my friends and neighbors have memories of her kindness. She never felt burdened or exhausted with all the work she did for us. She served with genuine unconditional love. Also, she never had feelings of hate towards my dad due to his alcoholism. She always saw the bright side of people. She always respected him and offered support, compassion, and kindness. My dad, too, has a great deal of reverence for her.

She was not only an excellent grandmother, but also an excellent mother-in-law, not only towards my dad but also towards my aunt.

My aunt (my maternal uncle's wife) is a gynecologist who runs her own hospital. When my aunt was working, my grandmother always helped in the kitchen. She ensured everyone had a hearty meal and took care of my nephews when they were young. Without my grandmother's unconditional love, my aunt would not be able to dedicate herself to managing her hospital.

2. Resilience:

During my father's alcoholic years, my mother went through substantial emotional turmoil, and we often had a somber atmosphere at home. However, my mother supported my father throughout. When my dad decided to quit alcohol, she stood beside him and attended Alcoholics Anonymous meetings with him. She genuinely loved him and cared for his recovery. Due to her resilience, unconditional love, and support from well-wishers, my father was free from alcohol within a year of deciding to quit.

3. Compassion:

It was monsoon season in India while I was still in college. A nearby creek was flooded near my parents' apartment. The water had entered the homes of people living in the slum near the creek where our house helper also lived. My mother and my friend's mother, who lived across from our apartment in a bungalow, decided to help the people affected by the flooding. My mom made them delicious meals while my friend's mom sheltered them in her home. She had a large hall attached to her home, and it was sufficient to support the people of the homes that were affected near the creek. As a child, witnessing my mother's and my friend's mother's compassion, courage, leadership, and kindness, I was filled with gratitude towards them.

4. Sportsmanship:

My daughter loves to participate in pageants. During these events, I have noticed that she was not only confident and won on the stage, but she was also a winner off stage. She helped many other contenders who needed help with their makeup. Girls of that age can at times be arrogant, competitive, and unwilling to help, but my daughter was shining with inner beauty as she helped others with a genuine feeling of kindness. She truly wins the Miss Inner Beauty title in my eyes for her kindness.

5. Sisterhood:

In my previous neighborhood, my neighbors and a few other ladies decided to get together and organize a vendor expo for all the neighboring women's small businesses. They genuinely cared for and helped each other. There was no competition, but only love towards helping women grow their businesses. A flyer was created, the expo was advertised, and everyone cheered each other. Kudos to these ladies for their spirit.

6. Empathy:

A few years ago, I had a mystery illness with my digestive system, and my weight dropped drastically. Also, I had to stop my car several times due to uneasy feelings of shakiness, which subsided after about 30 minutes. This went on for about 2.5 years. Doctors could not diagnose or treat this illness. In most instances when I had to stop the car, I used to call upon a friend for help. She always made herself available and came by rushing to help me. She genuinely cared and showed a great deal of empathy towards me. I will always be grateful for her unconditional love and support during my tough times. Similarly, I also had a kind neighbor friend who would always offer to drive my daughter to her dance lessons along with her daughter and offer to take me to the grocery store at times. Without the help of these selfless women, I would not be able to help myself back up.

7. Collaboration:

I facilitate self-esteem, confidence, and mindfulness workshops for children and women. One of my friends facilitates chess workshops and tournaments for children. She reached out to me to collaborate with her on summer camps. This is a win-win for both of us. We can offer more activities for children, and both our businesses can grow as a result. Similarly, recently, a few of the co-authors who shared the space with me for an anthology project decided to collaborate by inviting me to podcasts and interviews. I, too, decided to offer opportunities for them to volunteer at a non-profit I volunteer for, too. We do not know anything about each other's personal lives. We have never met before the project. However, each of us shares a genuine quality of helping other women succeed. Now, my sister and I are putting a course together and bringing our expertise to the table. It is fun to collaborate, give, and grow together. There is no greater joy than helping others win!

The world needs more women like these to win through kindness, compassion, and collaboration. True victory is helping others unconditionally and asking nothing in return. The only hindrance to being a true WINNER is ego, greed, and hate. To succeed, it is extremely important to keep our value systems and ego in check. It is said, "Keep your face always towards the sunshine, and shadows will fall behind you." Only if we have guiding values and principles outlined for ourselves will we move towards a better future. Values need to be instilled from childhood and witnessed through life experiences. If we cannot instill values in ourselves and others, the world will be a dead place. My mission and vision are to empower children, teens, and women with values, confidence, self-esteem, and emotional intelligence to move towards a compassionate world with clarity.

Hence, I would like to share this self-care routine that empowers and helps every woman win.

The Winning Self-Care Routine

Identify your values: Take time to identify your core values. Instill them in your beliefs, thoughts, feelings, words, and actions.

Identify your strengths: Identify your inner and outer strengths and work towards strengthening them further.

Identify your higher impersonal goals: Goals can be personal, and that's okay, but we need to move one step ahead and identify our impersonal goals. What can we give to make our family and this world a better place? Go beyond the "I" and focus on "Us."

Be grateful: Stay in gratitude every moment. Identify everything you can be grateful for every day and note it down in a gratitude journal.

Forgive: To err is human, but to forgive is divine. Let us try to make more space in our hearts for everyone. When we forgive, we create more space for love.

Let go: Let go of all the bitterness, hurt, negative emotions, and patterns that do not serve you, and make space for happiness, success, and prosperity to thrive.

Affirm: Write down affirmations that serve you and the world. Read them before going to bed.

Visualize: Visualize the outcome you desire through your goals. See yourself achieving your goals. Visualize success and feel as if it is already achieved.

Serve Selflessly: Service is not just volunteering in a non-profit. Service is responding to every human, animal, bird, and plant with kindness, compassion, gratitude, forgiveness, and humility.

The well-known leadership coach John Maxwell says, "Leaders become great not because of their power but because of their ability to empower others."

And to empower others, we must first empower ourselves through this self-care routine.

Let us make our lives count with a winning attitude. The world is waiting for us to lead with a grateful heart and arms wide open. Make This Life the Best One!

DK Hillard

Founder of DK Hillard Art, LLC
Artist, Designer & Author

https://www.linkedin.com/in/debra-hillard-93526913/
https://www.facebook.com/dkhillardart/
https://www.instagram.com/dkhillard/
https://www.dkhillard.com
https://www.dkhillardart.com

Debra is a creator. It is how she lives and what she does in her work. Her art has been a consistent thread throughout her life, whether it be painting, writing or working with others. It is based in her spiritual journey, her Shamanic practice and her connection to nature. For 20 years she was a life coach and personal trainer, a career that evolved out of her experience transforming her life through bodybuilding. During that time she developed a 12 week program using the body as a vehicle for transforming your entire life. She transforms her paintings into sensual, luxurious fabrics-clothing, blankets and pillows called "Wraptures", bringing the energy of her artwork into forms you can touch. They are filled with the love that she puts into everything she creates. She works with individuals and small groups using many of the interactive processes she developed while teaching her program.

Making the Choice to Thrive

By DK Hillard

Success is about more than business. It's about how I choose to live my life. The freedom to steer my own ship—to make every decision myself—has always been essential to me. Moving to the Southwest from a small town in New England almost thirty years ago was a bold choice, but it was driven by the desire to start anew, to create something out of a dream, and to face the unknown as I had so many times before.

During my years in New England, I faced significant health challenges. After spending a decade seeing doctors with no real answers or solutions, I realized I needed to take matters into my own hands. The experts told me that I would never lead a normal life again, be able to do physical exercise again, and never feel well again. I was nearing forty, too young to call it quits. It became clear that I had to regain my physical strength. So, I hired a strength coach from a local university to help guide me. The journey was long, often interrupted by weeks of being bedridden, but during those months in the gym, working closely with him, I gradually turned my health around.

As I progressed, I found myself becoming a mentor to many of the women in the gym. They watched me transform from being overweight, weak, and unable to do more than five minutes of exercise without collapsing, to someone who was strong and determined. By the eighth month of working with my coach, I made another self-loving decision: I was going to become a trainer myself. I wanted to help others transform their lives, just as training had transformed mine.

That decision set me on an entirely new path. By the time we were preparing for our move across the country, I was not only planning a fresh start, but also laying the groundwork for a new business.

Starting a training business in a new city where I had no connections meant I needed both a steady income and a clear vision. So, I found a way to stay physically active while building my business on the side. I created a house cleaning service, going door-to-door and leaving flyers everywhere I could. Slowly, I built up enough clients to support my family while I networked and developed the contacts I needed for my training business.

I organized my cleaning schedule to accommodate my training hours and used every available opportunity to connect with local businesses that might need my services. This period became one of my most creative in terms of marketing. I reached out to modeling agencies, offering to keep their models in shape. I partnered with physicians to promote preventive health. I gave talks at doctors' offices about the benefits of weight training. I attended networking meetings and made connections wherever I could. I gave free workshops on stress, diet, and exercise. People paid attention to my passion because it was evident that I was a walking example of the words I spoke.

The first training client I gained came as a surprise birthday gift from her husband, a man who worked out at the same gym as I did. I remember him telling me, "Those who have integrity will succeed here in Phoenix, because it's a rare trait in business." His wife, who struggled with diabetes and hated exercise, was furious when he bought her an at-home training package as a gift. But soon, we became great friends, and her health improved so much that she was nearly off insulin. I ended up training both of her daughters as well.

And that's how my business grew—by word of mouth. One person would rave about their experience with me, and then I'd get their friends and families. My clientele continued to expand, and I loved every minute of it.

Then, in February of 2000, the next big crash came—literally. My mother was visiting, and we were out for an afternoon together when an SUV ran a red light and hit us from the side. I tried to turn the wheel to avoid the collision, but it happened so quickly, there was nothing I could do. I heard the sickening sound of my arm breaking as the airbag deployed, followed by my screams. My mother's head slammed into the passenger door, and everything stopped. We were both in shock.

Ambulances rushed us to the hospital, and it wasn't until two days later, after surgery to insert a steel plate in my arm and multiple attempts to assess my mother's injuries, that I learned she would survive. She went home before me, but to a place where I knew she wouldn't receive proper care. My husband, unable to take charge, left my mother and son to manage on their own. I arrived home weak, shaken, and terrified, knowing that my ability to physically train was now uncertain. I had been the primary provider for our family, and without me, I feared we would lose everything we had built.

During my eighteen months of recovery, I had to face the fact that I might not be physically able to continue the work I had been doing. Unsure of the extent to which the accident had hindered my ability to use my right arm, I made a decision. I had to find another way to share my experience and training. And I also had to find a way to make a living. We were almost broke. With all of that looming over me and still facing the struggles of rehab, I developed a twelve-week transformational program called "Being Physical." Combining every bit of transformational work I had done over decades, with my years of study and experience as a trainer and life coach, I created a program using the body as a vehicle to transform your life. The first twelve participants gathered in my living room, ready to embark on an unknown journey. My business was called PhysioCentrics, The Art and Science of Physical Transformation. I had already begun to blend my creative vision with the science and business of training without realizing just how prophetic it was, and I was gently moving in the direction of being the artist I had always been.

I poured myself into those programs, into working with each and every individual. Sharing my own struggles and challenges, the things I did to overcome them, and all that I had learned along the way. I received more certifications so that I could better serve my clients, all while recovering from the accident. They saw me do my own work, and that inspired them to keep going with theirs. I was tough on myself; no excuses were adequate for giving up, and in turn, my clients leaned into the work required to reach their goals. They left bad marriages, started businesses, lost weight, got off medications, and went after dreams they had forgotten they had. Lives were changing all around me, but mine, as good as I felt about my work, was clearly in trouble.

The neglect and abuse I had put up with all my life, beginning in childhood and then in marriage, was no longer palatable. I made another decision. If nothing changed by the time I turned fifty, I was leaving. As I have said, being successful is as much about how I choose to live my life as it is about the business I create, and it is about how I use my choices to inspire and uplift others. It's about taking risks to make dreams come to fruition. It's about forging into the unknown without a lifeboat. I began to have a vision for myself and my life through the work I was doing with others, and I wanted more. I wanted more than I had ever allowed myself to believe possible. I knew that my choices were about more than they appeared to be on the surface. I was choosing life.

Fifty came and went. I divorced and started over, without a safety net. It was an act of self-love that eventually blossomed into a new relationship, a new beginning, and the support to pursue my passion. It took years. This didn't happen overnight, but what did happen was an opening of my heart to love. First, I had to love myself enough to receive what was offered. When I did, true love walked in the door. That led to a safe home, the support of someone who believed in me, and the ability to be the artist I had always been.

Now my passion flows and flourishes because I am learning to allow abundance to enter in many forms. I still have health challenges that require me to make difficult choices, and I make them knowing that they are an act of love and appreciation for myself. In loving myself and choosing to thrive, I send out ripples that touch the world, a silent act of love that embraces us all.

Feeling inspired by what you've just read and ready to explore further? I offer a transformative process to help you reconnect with the truth of who you are, creating unique and powerful anchors through my art. Reach out to me here to start your journey.

Kerrie D. Stone

Founder of SheThatExists
Minister, Metaphysician, Mystical Life Coach,
Visionary & Creative Director

https://www.linkedin.com/in/rev-kerrie-d-stone-a19964299/
https://www.facebook.com/shethatexists
https://www.instagram.com/shethatexiststheuniteroftribes/
https://shethatexists.com
https://kerriedstone.com

Kerrie D. Stone, Founder of SheThatExists, is a former child performer in dance/theater performance arts at Story Book Theater Playhouse in Texas. She is a former gymnast and has performed in parades. A former select corporate softball athlete, she has played several team sports. She is a musician trained in clarinet, piano, and the xylophone, having performed in concert and jazz bands. She is an awarded esthetician. A former showwoman, she produced her own community show as a single mom. Born a spiritual child, she professed her faith in Creator at age 15. A champion in supporting others in their greatness, she has 36 years of team/leadership experience. Today she is an Ordained Minister in service of life as sacred, a mystical life coach, metaphysician, visionary, wisdom teacher, polymath, Creative Director, and Comedian. Her favorite passion is being momma. She is earning her Masters degree and is a PhD candidate.

A Look Back: A Life Well Lived from the heart as soul - The Making of a Winner

By Kerrie D. Stone

When I was a child and young teenager, one of the most vivid memories that I have is my mom and sister ganging up on me and calling me a brat. It was very confusing to me because my mom was supposed to be my mom, and my sister was older, and I always loved her very dearly and looked up to her as my older sister. I look back now and realize this was and is mental, emotional, and spiritual abuse.

I remember when I was twelve or thirteen years old, there was a bully in the neighborhood named Megan. She was so mean. She bullied me all the time. She was not nice at all. I didn't understand why people could be so mean to others, especially at such a young age; however, now that I'm older and I have a Mastery in Consciousness and am earning my Master's degree in the Psychology of Consciousness and have sought truth and wisdom in my life, I can see more clearly why people act the way that they do. I remember that my dad told me that the only way to stand up to a bully was to fight them. I remember my dad sent me to walk down past Megan's house and to bring my sister; I was terrified. Megan was so mean and scary—she was very big and intimidating. Today, I do not agree with my dad. According to Exodus 14:14, God fights our battles for us. I do not agree that the only way to stand up to a bully is to fight them. Today, I know that a great way to stand up to a bully and a mean person is simply to voice and tell the truth about them or to write about them truthfully, openly, and honestly. In this way, when you stand up for your Self and speak for your Self, you can also tell who the followers are who fall in line with the bullies and the mean people. I see so many broken and weak adults today who are terrified of standing up and doing the right thing. This should not be the norm.

When I was in High School, I was a lone wolf, except for my friends that I had in church and a couple of people that I sat next to in my classes. I started to see and notice that everyone was a part of a "click" and if someone was not part of that "click," then these girls who were a part of the "click" treated other girls very poorly and were mean. This was before the *Mean Girls* movie with Lindsay Lohan came out. I look back and am so grateful I was never that mean girl in high school and that I shared the love of God that lives in my heart.

I gave my life to God at 15 in a real way, and so I never cared to be a part of any "clicks" in High School, and I didn't care about being "popular" at all in any way. I've never cared about being popular. As a child of God, I always wanted to share the love of God that lived in me and tell people how much God loves them. I had people make fun of me in High School, calling me "Bible Girl." I didn't know they were making fun of me and bullying me because I was so full of the love of God. I went to a public school, and looking back, I wonder if my life would have been better if I had gone to a private school or faith-based school.

Once I graduated from High School, I began my journey in college and full-time work for the Post Office. I had an experience with a guy friend that was not so great: he started out nice, and then his true "grey" came out. I didn't have a relationship with my parents that was nurturing and loving, so I did not have a strong basis for what a healthy relationship was versus a non-healthy relationship. I was 18 and knew nothing about life and didn't have a good foundation on how the world was because my parents never taught me and never shared wisdom with me in a loving way and threw me out to the wolves in sheep's clothing as soon as I graduated from High School and even worse, they moved states away and I felt so abandoned. Thank goodness, I had God.

I was mentally, emotionally, physically, and spiritually abused in my home environment, so I had confusion about what was healthy and what was not healthy. I also did not know that I did not have to tolerate guy friends being that way. A part of me thought I had to stay in an abusive friendship with a guy and thought that it was normal. I think I stopped talking to my guy friend Eric after he spit in my face and broke into my apartment when I was not home and turned the temperature in my apartment all the way up so when I got home from work my apartment door was open and unlocked for anyone to break into and the temperature was like 90 degrees. I did not have a relationship with my parents, meaning they were not safe people in my life that I could talk to, and I remember just being so confused about life.

Somehow God saved me from that "friend" and I was able to get away, move back "home" with my parents after much begging and pleading, and move forward with my life so I didn't get stuck in an abusive relationship were I thought I had to stay and be abused by someone who wasn't really a true friend. My parents never explained to me anything about abusive relationships in that way. When I look back on that situation, I wonder if he thought he could be mean to me because I was so kind, compassionate, heart-centered, loving, and nice. This is why it's important to create healthy boundaries and not let people be mean to us or hurt us mentally, emotionally, or spiritually.

When I look back at life, one of the meanest people that I have ever met in my life, other than some of my own family members, is my former husband's now ex-girlfriend. Her name is Kelsy. (Don't worry, sometimes an author has to change the names to protect the guilty party.) 😊

My husband apparently got into a relationship with Kelsy when we were still married. My husband was with Kelsy for over ten years and never married her. She was so mean to me. She is still very mean today at the time of this writing. Other than some of my own family members, I had no idea that anyone could be so mean to anyone. It seems surreal. I look back today and I realize that she was jealous and envious of me because I had what she could never have, and that is a kind, loving, and genuine heart as a true soul. I also had a child with Scott, my former husband, and that is something she could never have. I look back and see that she was even jealous and envious of my daughter. She hated my and my daughter's pure, undefiled, and non-adulterated bond. I still have all of the messages that Kelsy would message me in Facebook Messenger when I would reach out to her concerning my daughter after I survived my former husband's domestic terrorism and hate on my life when he decided to use our only child as a pawn of war to break me and to financially devastate me and do everything he could to destroy my life, and his attempts forced me into a life of homelessness and destitution back in 2016. It would have happened, but God used a kind man to save me, who told me to "pay it forward" regarding all the help and financial support he gave me to stay alive and safe off the streets, since I didn't have a car to sleep in, until I could rebuild my life with the help of God.

Kelsy called me every bad name in the book and she made up lies and rumors about me saying that I was a prostitute and that I was on meth. I could not believe that my own husband would get with someone like this or even bring our daughter around someone like this. She obviously did not care about setting a good example to her own daughter, who was a few years older than my daughter. She took my husband down to the bottom of the barrel of life spiritually. She did not make him a better person. She did not help him to become whole spiritually. He still has not recovered today. I realized that if she talked to me like this, then she definitely was spiritually, mentally, and emotionally abusing my daughter all the time. Kelsy is not with my daughter's dad today; she is with someone else. She is still abusive. She tries to gaslight me and tell me that I have no education and no degrees, even though I have an Esthetics degree, an Associate's degree in Arts, a Mastery in Consciousness, and a Bachelor's degree in the Metaphysical Sciences, which is a non-secular degree in higher education. I'm earning my Master's degree as well in the Psychology of Consciousness. I don't think she has any degrees. I tried to help encourage her in helping her have the confidence to start and build her own business teaching people about successful bartending because she is a lifelong bartender.

When I was in my thirties, I remember my sister bullying me and trying to violate my rights as a mom to lawfully homeschool my daughter, and trying to protect my daughter from being abused in school. Homeschooling my daughter was my original intention when my daughter's dad and I decided to start a life and family together, so I was taking steps to do what God wanted me to do originally. My sister got her PTA "friends" to gossip about me. My sister also had her female friends gang up on me with gossip and ostracizing me. She made sure that the moms in the small town that we lived in did not invite me to the keno group, and she made sure that they did not support my small custom clothing and scarf business that I started to create extra income as a single mom. I had a mom cancel their order and tell me that they could not buy a custom-made scarf from me because my sister told them she would not be friends with them anymore if they purchased a custom scarf from me. My sister spent many years sabotaging my life in many different ways.

Other than that, I can think of one other mean girl named Jordan who was seriously mean. She hated me because I was becoming "popular" as a performance artist and creative director in my 30s. I successfully organized and directed my own live community show. Jordan was a singer and played some instruments, and I remember how jealous and envious she was of me. She would bully me and try to start fights with me, intimidate me, and scare me when we were at the same events. She would try to get her female friend to gang up on me with her. Thank goodness, I kept walking away, not entangling my Self with her. I'm sure God protected me from her. I later heard from one of her other friends that Jordan would do black magic and try to put curses on me, and apparently she was a practicing "dark magic" witch, and she was so jealous and envious of me that she wanted me dead.

Other than that, there was this female named Sheryl (names changed to protect the guilty) who was flat-out nasty to me. Sheryl started all kinds of rumors about me, but in reality none of them were true and she was just covering for the fact that she was letting an older guy in his late 30s in a school that we attended sexualize, groom, and be in a sexual relationship with her twelve/thirteen-year-old daughter, and it all came to light and she tried to blame me for it because I was the one who approached my teacher about it and confronted the situation after some other people asked me about what was going on in that situation because they saw her daughter kissing my teacher. She "spiritualized" the situation and said that they were together in a past life, and that's what made it okay for them to be together in that way in this lifetime; people bought into it. She was so mean to me after I discovered who she really was; before that, she was always very fake "nice" and was always "love bombing" me to try to make herself look spiritual. Because of this, I learned to pray for discernment and ask God to show me people's true intentions.

For years, I stayed silent with all the bullying and abuse I endured from mean people. God told me to stay silent. I never retaliated, and I never stooped to their low level and low vibration that these mean females carried. Over the years, I have been privileged enough to come to know God as my protector and sustainer. This is something that I have in my relationship with God that I know is very valuable that these other mean girls don't have. This is something that those mean girls can't take away from me.

"The Lord God is a sun, a shield:
the Lord will give us his favor and glory."—Psalm 84

I share this because it is important to know that we can get what we want and have a good life without being mean. It is very important to be compassionate and loving to others. I have provided a very good example to my niece and daughter to not be hateful to others and to be a compassionate presence for those in a time when someone may need care and comfort. I look back at my life and realize how important it is to show people the love of God. We never know how sharing the love of God or sharing goodness and compassion with another can save a life. People commit suicide for a lot of reasons these days. People commit suicide because they are bullied. I know it is God who protected me from Kelsy when she would abuse me with my daughter and use my daughter as a pawn in a war for her own selfish gain.

We want to be a reason why others feel safe and supported in life. It is important to be a presence in someone's life that is supportive and caring. It is important to lift others up, and we should never beat anyone down with our words. We should always help others when they need help or are in need. Our world is really backwards when it comes to this. We are called to be the living body of Christ our Selves, not a government organization. When we show up for people and give, we never know if we are going to save that person's life or not. It is really important to stand up for others. We must be willing to stand alone and to always do what is right, even when everyone around us is bowing to the ways of the world and turning a blind eye to the basic needs of others. We are called to give to those who have need. We are called to love others in a real, actionable, and tangible way. When we do this, to me, this is winning.

> *"We must live life as a gift to be given to others-*
> *not a treasure to be kept."*—Pope Francis

I have never retaliated against any of my haters. I have learned that God is my protector—he fights for me on my behalf and is my present help at all times. Telling the truth about people is important.

This is the best way to take care of ourSelves unless God calls us to stay silent for certain reasons, then God will always protect us. It took me years to find my true soul's voice and to listen to God to protect me in the meantime.

I've learned that my God given gift of gentleness is one of my greatest strengths. I still get misunderstood in life, and that is okay. God works out everything for me. We don't live in a world that is healed and whole, so there are going to be many obstacles and hurdles in life.

If you have the gift of gentleness like I do, I encourage you with everything that is alive in me to stay gentle. Do not ever let the world take your gentle nature from you, or try to make you harden your heart. Protect your gentle nature with everything you have and do not change for anyone. Gentleness is a superpower. I know because my gentleness is a superpower. It is not a weakness. It is a powerful superpower from the Creator. Gentleness is power and strength under control.

"We are each of us angels with one wing. And we can only fly embracing each other."—Luciano De Crescenzo

It is important that we speak life into others. We are called to stand up for those who don't have a voice and who are not able to take up for themselves. One of the first messages that God gave me to share on my YouTube channel, SheThatExists HerStory, is called "This one is for the voiceless." In this message, I take up for those who do not have a voice, who are unable to voice for themselves because it is not safe for them. I invite you to go check it out.

As far as winning...

Sometimes winning is just knowing that at the end of the day we have not caused intentional harm and damage to someone and that we can go to bed and sleep at night with clean hands and a clean heart. It is really important to listen to your God-gifted conscience. I know so many people who have lost their God or Creator-gifted conscience because they turned a blind eye to it for so long.

It is interesting that we all get along with each other in kindergarten and then all of a sudden, so many are filled with so much hate and treat each other so poorly. We are called to support those who have less, and we are called to support those and give to those in need. Being nice and compassionate is not a weakness. It is a gift from God that is valuable and should be treated as such. Having a truly good heart is becoming rarer these days. Giving directly to others and being generous can save a life, and when we give, it will always come back to us in a different form when we need it.

As far as finishing first...

Life is a gift and our lives are sacred. It is important to walk in life with integrity and a good heart. People forget about their inner child and their own innocence, and that is too bad. I don't know if remaining true to my inner child and my true Self as a true soul has caused me to finish "first." I do know that I have a clean heart and a clean conscience, and I'm able to sleep at night in a very deep, peaceful way. What people don't know is that the law of sowing and reaping is very real. This is something that folks need to consider.

We have too many broken adults bullying and being mean to others and ganging up on people who they deem as weak just because they are kind, caring, or loving to others. I share this chapter to encourage the mean, broken adults and mean females to consider going deeper into why they have to hurt others mentally, emotionally, and spiritually. When I die, and while I am very much alive, I want my niece and my daughter to know that I lived/live a life of love, goodness, and service filled with compassionate action. I want them to know that I left a legacy of love, goodness, and service to them and to those in need. It's always important that we communicate with others if there ever is a falling out or miscommunication. Apologizing to someone is important. Authenticity is important. Sharing from your heart is important. Extending the olive branch of peace is important when we have miscommunication with others.

When you get older in life, you start to realize who your true friends are. We should never try to fit in just to get accepted. It is more than okay to walk alone and to be an individual. It is vital in life to be true to your Self and trust that God will bring the right people into your life at the right time. When we share the love of God and be the love of God, fully embodying God's love and being able to share and express God's love and goodness to others—that is finishing first. God seems to take care of the rest. We can't purchase peace in our hearts—this is something that is priceless. Keep being a loving individual, and the right people will come into your life and support you on your journey to your highest calling and purpose in life. This is how it has happened for me, even through the deepest despair and deepest heartache.

God protected me and always sent the right people into my life at the right time. I want to encourage you that God will do that for you as well. Never be afraid to feel your feelings and emotions; suppression never helps. Suppressing our feelings and emotions actually separates us from our divine nature, the totality of our human existence. That is for another chapter or story and for another time. Life is sacred. To be continued. ☺

> *"God's light can shine in the most hidden corners of our lives."*
> —Pope Francis

I hope this encourages those who read it. Stay the course. Even in the darkest of times, God will send the right people to bring light into your life and bring kind, loving, and beautiful heart-centered people into your life when you need it most.

Psalm 23.

Natalie Horseman

Horseman Publishing

https://www.instagram.com/horsemanpenandprose/
https://www.horsemanbooks.com

Natalie Horseman, MSN, RN, is a dedicated nurse with nearly two decades of experience in child and family development. Her extensive background in healthcare has equipped her with a profound understanding of resilience and strength. Throughout her career, Natalie has been committed to guiding individuals through life's most challenging moments with both compassion and empathy. Her personal journey of overcoming adversity has deeply fueled her passion for empowering others. Through her writing, Natalie combines practical advice with heartfelt encouragement, creating a sense of community for those navigating life's storms. She believes that while our experiences shape us, they do not define us. Through her contributions, Natalie strives to inspire readers to embrace their inner strength and resilience, offering reassurance that they are never alone on their journey.

The Permission Slip

By Natalie Horseman

The Price of Putting Others First

For most of my life, I've put others' needs before my own. Whether it was supporting friends, family, or colleagues, I always thought that prioritizing others was the right thing to do. It felt natural to make sure everyone else was happy, healthy, and fulfilled, even if it meant sacrificing my own happiness in the process. I thought my worth came from being helpful, kind, and selfless, but in reality, I lost touch with who I was and what I needed.

By constantly thinking about the impact on others, I suppressed my own voice. I didn't ask for help, stopped acknowledging my desires, and started feeling disconnected from my true self. As a result, I became more silent, both figuratively and literally. I didn't speak up for my needs, let alone pursue my dreams. I had learned to be "nice," but I'd forgotten how to be true to myself.

The truth is, I had been living with the assumption that putting others first would ultimately lead to my own happiness. But in the process, I was drowning in self-doubt, never considering what I truly wanted, and finding it harder and harder to say "yes" to my own dreams.

The Turning Point

After years of feeling like I was losing myself, I realized something had to change. So, I began the challenging work of self-discovery. Therapy was my first step in this new direction. It wasn't easy; confronting the ways I had neglected my own needs and suppressed my voice was painful. But through therapy, I came to understand that it wasn't selfish to put myself first, that my dreams and desires were just as important as anyone else's.

I learned the power of boundaries—how saying "no" was just as important as saying "yes." I also realized that I had spent my adult life feeling unworthy of good things because I'd always put others before myself. The work wasn't just about learning how to communicate my needs—it was about learning to believe I was worth those needs being met.

This period of self-reflection ultimately gave me the clarity to recognize that it was time to focus on my own dreams. For 20 years, I had wanted to write a children's book. It had always been something I put aside, something I didn't think I could do. But as I learned to prioritize myself, I realized that it was finally time to take action on this dream.

The Dream Deferred

For two decades, I thought about writing a children's book, but I always found a reason to wait. I wasn't ready. I wasn't sure I could do it. My inner critic was loud, telling me I didn't have the skill, the time, or the experience to create something others would enjoy.

Then, one day, I sat down at my desk and began to write. It wasn't pretty. The words were unpolished, the story meandered, and it felt unfinished. But it was something. I had done it. The rough draft was messy, but it was a start. And that was the most important part—getting it down on paper.

There's something incredibly empowering about just beginning, even when the result isn't perfect. For years, I'd been waiting for the "right" moment, for everything to be aligned. But the truth was, the right moment doesn't exist. It's about showing up, putting in the work, and trusting that progress will come, even if it's imperfect.

Learning the Craft

After completing my first draft, I realized that my journey was only just beginning. Writing a children's book wasn't as simple as putting words on a page. I had to learn about the craft—structure, pacing, word count, and understanding the target audience. To do this, I enrolled in a writing class to better understand what makes a children's book truly engaging.

The lessons from that class were more than technical—they were personal. I had to learn to trust the process, to accept that growth comes from stepping outside of my comfort zone, and to realize that it was okay to ask for help.

From Procrastination to Publication

Even after completing my rough draft and taking the writing class, I hesitated. The fear of rejection, failure, and not being "good enough" crept in. I let the manuscript sit untouched for nine months, questioning whether it was worth pursuing at all.

But in 2024, something changed. I wrote down my goals for the year, and right at the top, front and center, was the goal to be a published author. I wasn't sure how to get there, but I knew I had to move forward. Writing it down made it real—it gave me something tangible to work toward.

Vision boards had never been my thing, but seeing my goal every day was powerful. It kept me accountable, kept me focused. And slowly, I started to believe that maybe I could do this. I began revising the manuscript and reached out to publishers. And then, something incredible happened—I finally saw my book in print.

Saying Yes to Me

The feeling of holding that published book in my hands was indescribable. It was surreal, but also incredibly fulfilling. For so long, I had held back from saying "yes" to my dreams, convinced that I wasn't worthy of this accomplishment. But as I saw the positive feedback from children, parents, and even fellow authors, I began to realize that the journey was worth it.

Since publishing my children's book, I've had the honor of contributing to two other anthologies. These opportunities have been incredible, allowing me to connect with like-minded individuals and grow in my craft. The creative doors that have opened to me have brought unexpected joy, community, and fulfillment.

Believing in myself and saying "yes" to my dream didn't just change my life—it opened up a world of possibilities I never could have imagined. I've learned that being kind and putting others first is still a strength—but only when it comes from a place of self-fulfillment rather than self-sacrifice. Now, I give to others without losing myself in the process, knowing that true kindness includes extending that same compassion to myself.

The Winding Road

Looking back, I realize how much self-doubt held me back. It kept me small, in the shadows, afraid of stepping into the light. The journey to believing in myself has been long and filled with challenges, but it has been worth every single step.

I know the road to self-belief isn't easy. It's bumpy, uncertain, and sometimes, it feels like you've hit a dead end. But the wonderful thing is that you can always create a new path. Dreams don't have to happen in a straight line—they can be messy, they can take detours, and they can take years to come to fruition. But if you keep going, eventually, you'll get there.

It's never too late to say "yes" to your dreams, to prioritize yourself, and to find your voice. You deserve it, and so much more.

Five Tips to Move Forward with Confidence

1. **Start Small**
    Break your big dreams into small, manageable steps. Focus on one action at a time—each step brings you closer to your goal.

2. **Embrace Imperfection**
    Don't wait for perfection. Your first draft, idea, or attempt doesn't have to be flawless—progress is more important than perfection.

3. **Speak Up for Your Needs**
    Don't suppress your voice. Start by expressing your needs, whether in personal relationships or projects, and remember, it's okay to ask for help.

4. **Surround Yourself with Support**
    Find people who uplift and encourage you. Positive support can fuel your belief in yourself and help you stay motivated.

5. **Trust the Journey**
    Believe that every challenge serves a purpose. Even when things feel uncertain, trust that the journey will teach you what you need to grow.

Your Path

If you've ever felt like your dreams were out of reach, or that you didn't have the courage to say "yes" to yourself, know that you're not alone. The road is challenging, but it's yours to navigate. Trust that the journey is worth it. Keep pushing forward, and remember that you are capable of creating your own path, no matter how long it takes. The only permission you need to chase your dreams is your own. And today, I hope you say "yes."

Fernanda Lima Firman

Brezze.AI
AI Strategist and Coach for Business

https://www.linkedin.com/in/felimafirman/
https://www.facebook.com/fefirman/
https://www.instagram.com/fernanda.firman/
https://brezze.ai
https://www.fernandafirman.com

Fernanda Lima Firman is a Brazilian architect turned Business Profit Architect, AI Automation Strategist, and Business Marketing Expert. She helps women in business simplify their systems, amplify their impact, and scale with ease. As the founder of Brezze, an AI-powered marketing agency, Fernanda supports coaches, course creators, and service providers with smart automation, high-converting marketing strategies, and profitable virtual events—without tech overwhelm or burnout. She's the creator of an AI-driven CRM that streamlines lead generation, sales, and client onboarding, so women can grow their businesses and reclaim their time. With over 50 successful launches and events under her belt, Fernanda's Business Profit Architecture™ Blueprint has helped clients boost visibility, build authority, and convert leads on autopilot. Her mission is simple: help women build scalable businesses that align with their values and support the life they truly want. ☞ Book your free audit call at www.fernandafirman.com/audit

Purpose Found Me

By Fernanda Lima Firman

It started at a restaurant in my small hometown, where Ana leaned across the table and said, "I met someone."

"Really? Who?" I asked.

"You don't know him... He's American."

I was surprised. "Where did you meet an American?"

She hesitated before answering, "On the internet."

I stared at her, confused. "What's that? Is it a place?"

She laughed. "No. It's on the computer. There's this site—Christian Café. You can meet people who share your faith in the United States."

Internet access was rare then. She invited me to her house that weekend to show me. We created a profile out of curiosity.

That's how I met Sam.

He was an architect in California. I was an architect in Brazil. Our first messages were about work. He asked if I wanted to help with designs, and we began collaborating remotely.

Over time, our conversations shifted from professional to personal. One day, he asked what I found most attractive in a man.

"Hands," I said without hesitation.

"Mine are beautiful," he replied quickly.

Later, he said a client wanted to meet the woman behind the work and offered to bring me to California to finalize the project. He framed it as business, but by then, I knew it was more.

In December 2003, I boarded a flight to Los Angeles. I didn't come to chase a dream. I came to finish a project.

But I stepped into something entirely different.

Sam was waiting when I arrived. We recognized each other immediately, with a quiet familiarity built over months of conversations.

The moment he reached for my bag, I noticed what he had never mentioned: he was missing a thumb.

Weeks earlier, when he claimed his hands were beautiful after I shared what I found attractive, he'd chosen to lie. That first lie left a mark. I said nothing, but something in me tightened.

His house felt cold and unwelcoming, but I was still adjusting after traveling across the world to meet someone I barely knew outside a screen. I kept telling myself we were just getting to know each other.

At first, I thought he was being helpful by driving me places, waiting outside, always close. But that quickly felt like surveillance. I couldn't go anywhere alone. I wasn't allowed to make friends. I had no phone or car. When I worked on client designs, he kept all the money, claiming it was "for us."

He began speaking for me in conversations, answering questions before I could. When I asked for anything—a phone, space, money—he'd dismiss me or trigger guilt. Every concern somehow became my fault.

"You're overreacting," he'd say. "You don't understand how things work here."

I started shrinking into silence. I stopped asking.

He told me about his ex-wife trying to take his son away for money and spite. He claimed she falsely painted him as an abuser, forcing supervised visitation. The system was against him, he said, and I was the only person he could trust.

I believed and helped him.

Then, he announced we were getting married—not as a question, but as a decision already made.

"I love you," he said. "And I know you love me, too. You just don't know it yet."

By then, I had no support network, no friends, no income. I was completely dependent, and he knew it.

One evening, he handed me a document. "This is just a formality," he explained. "A prenuptial agreement."

The contract I signed had been written by his lawyer and translated into Portuguese. I didn't have a lawyer. I wasn't after his money and was proud of what I'd built in Brazil.

The prenup showed he was a millionaire with properties throughout Santa Monica, not a property manager as he told me.

Another lie I justified as if he just wanted to make sure I loved him for who he was.

As I reviewed the document, his birthdate caught my eye. He had told me he was ten years older than I. The prenup revealed he was seventeen years older.

Another lie.

When I looked at him, hoping for an explanation, he said, "I hadn't told you the truth because I was afraid you wouldn't come."

I felt my body disconnect from my thoughts. He was calmly explaining another deception while somehow making me feel guilty.

On the wedding morning, I sat at a nail salon trying to feel something—joy, excitement, anything resembling love.

The manicurist looked up and smiled. "You're getting married today?"

I nodded.

"Are you happy?" she asked.

Looking down at my hands, I answered, "I don't know."

She tilted her head. "Don't go," she said gently. "That's not joy. That's your soul crying."

I wanted to cry harder then but stayed quiet.

We had no celebration. He said he'd already had a big wedding before and didn't want another. But it would have been my first.

He didn't want to spend money, so I never got to dream about a dress, and I wore a white dress from a graduation ceremony.

I drove myself to the ceremony in a car he salvaged from a junkyard. I remember sitting behind the wheel, veil on, seeing people glance at me through the windows. No one else was in the car. No flowers. No music. Just me.

After the ceremony, I asked if we could invite a couple I knew to dinner. He refused initially but later agreed. When the check came, he wouldn't pick it up. It sat there while everyone at the table grew quiet.

That's when I knew—not just that something was wrong, but that I had made a mistake.

At his house, I lived like a ghost. When I asked for space to keep my things and work, he brought me to the attic. No windows. Low ceiling. Stale air. It wasn't a space for living, but it became the only place where I could keep what was left of who I was.

One day at a women's clinic, I noticed a pamphlet titled "What Is Domestic Violence?" I picked it up and started reading. It listed signs I hadn't named—emotional abuse, financial control, isolation, surveillance. It was as if someone had written my life in bullet points.

The only thing missing was physical violence. He pinned me down in the attic once when I asked for my money, and I thought that was my last day. Then, I realized he couldn't afford to cross that line yet because of his custody battle. He wasn't protecting me. He was using me as his cover story.

At the bottom of the pamphlet was a phone number. I called.

A woman answered in a calm voice. She asked questions. Then, after I told her my story, she said, "You're in a dangerous situation. We can help you."

I said yes. That yes, it was the beginning of my exit plan.

With help from a trusted neighbor, I made arrangements. Quietly, I packed essentials into trash bags. I had no suitcase. No money of my own.

Before he left that morning, something felt off. I didn't trust he'd stay gone, so I called my sister in Brazil and asked her to stay on the phone. If I went silent, she was to call the police.

Then, he came back.

He stood in the doorway, expression sharp and cold, looking past me at the bags.

My heart raced, but I didn't waver. "If I hang up," I told him, "my sister will call the police."

He stared, and for a moment, I didn't know what he would do.

"I just want to leave," I said. "Let me go."

He stepped aside.

I threw everything into the car and drove to a safe location where someone from the shelter met me. I walked into the shelter with trash bags, a broken heart, and the quiet belief that somehow, God still had a plan.

The first shelter was heavy—early curfew, donated food, and air thick with fear. What broke me most were the children—moving through the shelter like shadows, silent and anxious. They weren't just surviving violence; they were learning to live without space to dream.

The mothers—strong, resilient, and kind—felt powerless. They couldn't work while under protection. Couldn't provide. Couldn't rebuild.

Those moments planted a seed for something I'd build much later.

One evening, I called my mother in Brazil.

"Why don't you try San Diego?" she suggested. "You have a friend there."

I refused. Starting over again seemed impossible.

Minutes later, the psychologist pulled me aside. "Fernanda, he found you. We have to release you."

I froze. "I have nowhere to go."

"There's nothing I can do," she said.

I began packing with no plan, believing I might sleep on the street.

But the psychologist returned. "I made some calls. There's a shelter in San Diego. They can take you."

And I knew: the door I had just refused was the one God had already opened.

When I arrived in San Diego, something shifted. A calm settled in my chest like a weight lifted. This shelter was different. Bright. Safe. I had my own room, clean bathrooms, and space to breathe. I could walk to the beach and pray. I had computer access to finish my master's degree. I was still healing, but here, I could hear my own voice again.

One week before my 30 days ended, I passed an architecture firm and said to myself, *I want to work there.*

The next day, I returned in a suit with my résumé. They called for an interview and offered me the job starting in 40 days. The perfect timing!

I left the shelter the day my father arrived from Brazil. But Sam had come with him, having tricked my family with promises of change. During my father's visit, we stayed in one of Sam's Santa Monica properties.

I agreed to one therapy session. Sam dominated the conversation, twisted my words, and won over the therapist. That experience cemented my decision.

Days later, my father flew home. I returned to San Diego. The next morning, I started my new job.

Before he left, he helped me find a roommate, a man, for safety. After three months, my roommate increased the rent beyond what I could afford. The night before flying to Brazil for Christmas, I searched Craigslist for other options.

Eric responded with unexpected kindness. He was also leaving town for the holidays, making the timing perfect.

When I returned, I moved in with Eric. One month later, we were dating.

Today, after fourteen years of marriage and two beautiful sons, I found my purpose: a podcast, "Raising Young Entrepreneurs." The idea comes directly from what I witnessed in those shelters: mothers trapped in cycles of dependence, unable to provide sustainable futures for their children. I hope to give parents tools to teach their children financial independence from an early age, so they never feel trapped by economic circumstances, and give women the tools they need to become financially free.

This story isn't about what was taken from me.

It's about doors that closed so the right ones could open.

It's about **how purpose found me** in the quiet moments between prayers, not because I chased it, but because I finally stood still enough to receive it.

Sometimes, purpose doesn't knock. It whispers. And we find it when we dare to listen.

Nikki Hillhouse

nikkihillhouse.com
Mindset and Therapeutic coach

https://www.linkedin.com/in/nikki-hillhouse-a6b25529b/
https://www.facebook.com/nikki.hillhouse.1
https://www.instagram.com/nikkihillhouse/
https://www.nikkihillhouse.com/

Nikki is an experienced Mind Detox Practitioner, Meditation Teacher, Well-being Coach, and Retreat Facilitator with a deep passion for holistic healing. With an extensive background in holistic health, she believes true Health, Wealth, Relationships, and Success come from aligning with our authentic selves. A Stroke-Thriver, Nikki has transformed her life from chronic pain and struggle to vibrant health and purpose. Her journey led her to the peaceful shores of beautiful Turkey, where she now lives and hosts transformational wellness retreats and runs a thriving coaching business. Her mission is to empower others to overcome their greatest challenges, transcend fears, and step into a life of freedom, happiness, health, and fulfillment. With a great passion is to help clients reconnect with their intuition, heal past wounds, and embrace their worthiness. Through her holistic approach, Nikki guides individuals toward self-discovery, resilience, and personal transformation, inspiring them to create a life without limits.

Rolling with the Dice—Negotiating Life's Unpredictable Path

By Nikki Hillhouse

For as long as I can remember, I played it safe; the quiet, sensitive soul who retreated into her own world, striving to meet everyone's needs before her own, believing that kindness meant getting everything right, staying quiet, and putting others first. Shaping my life around keeping the peace, convinced that staying small was the safest way to navigate an unpredictable world. I thought that by being the "good girl," doing everything for everyone else, avoiding conflict, and maintaining control over the chaos that seemed to surround me.

But life doesn't always unfold as expected. It has a way of throwing curveballs, forcing us to confront the very things we've been avoiding. Life, in all its unpredictability, had more to teach me than I ever could have imagined.

From Girl to Guardian: A Mother's Unseen Strength

At just 16, motherhood arrived unexpectedly. One moment, I was a teenager caught between childhood and adulthood, struggling with my own identity; the next, being responsible for another life. The shift was instantaneous, and I found myself desperately trying to juggle the demands of growing up and becoming a mother.

I was determined to be the best mother possible, proving that I could do it, despite being young. But in the process, I began to lose touch with the essence of who I was. The weight of responsibility was overwhelming, and in trying to be everything to everyone, I forgot to take care of myself.

Burying my own needs beneath the weight of responsibility, believing that love meant sacrifice. Working tirelessly to be everything for everyone, yet no matter how much I gave, it never felt like enough. I was always exhausted, always on the verge of burnout, and despite my efforts, I felt like I was failing. The constant feeling of inadequacy crept in, and loneliness became a companion. Longing for something more, but I didn't even know what that "more" was. I couldn't even put it into words, only that something deep within me was missing.

What I didn't understand at the time was that true self-worth doesn't come from what we give to others. It comes from knowing that we are enough, just as we are, and that we deserve to care for ourselves as much as we care for those we love.

The Moment That Changed Everything

At 31, my body demanded attention. I sought treatment for neck pain, convinced I was doing the "right" thing. I never imagined that an osteopathic manipulation could lead to a vertebral artery dissection, causing a life-changing stroke.

I remember the moment vividly. I was soaking in the bath, hoping to relieve the discomfort in my neck, when a wave of nausea and dizziness struck me. Then, out of nowhere, a blinding pain tore through my head. My limbs were heavy and unresponsive. My breath became shallow, and I couldn't move. I was alone and terrified, unsure of what was happening. But deep down, I knew it was serious.

When the doctor's words hit me, "stroke," it felt like the ground shifted beneath me. I had always been healthy, active, and full of energy. How could this happen to me? The fear of the unknown gripped me, and I couldn't grasp the reality of it. I had done everything "right," so why was I facing this? It didn't make sense.

The weight of the word "stroke" pressed down on me, and a flood of questions rushed in: *Will I ever be the same again? Will I be able to care for myself or my loved ones?* The uncertainty felt unbearable. It was clear that nothing would ever be the same again, and the path ahead was completely unknown. The life I had known was slipping away, and all I could do was try to face whatever was coming, no matter how terrifying it seemed.

The days and weeks that followed were a whirlwind of emotions: uncertainty, fear, and countless unanswered questions. Would life ever return to what it once was? The unknown felt heavy, like something precious had been lost and not just health, but a sense of self. My reflection in the mirror felt unfamiliar, almost like looking at a stranger. What I couldn't have known then was that, in time, this moment would become the catalyst for an extraordinary transformation. Recovery would prove to be about so much more than physical healing; it would become a journey of rediscovery, a chance to reconnect with the very essence of who I was, always there, waiting to be found.

The Power of Choosing Yourself

For 15 years, I minimised my pain, pushing through, and convincing myself I was fine. But I wasn't. My body was weak, the pain relentless, and the emotional toll overwhelming. On the darkest days, I questioned if I could continue. How could I go on when I felt so broken?

Then, in one of my darkest moments, something changed. As I lay in bed, weighed down by it all, I heard a voice, not from anyone around me, but from deep within. It wasn't external; it had always been there, patiently waiting for me to finally listen.

"Take your power back."

At first, it made no sense. Power? I didn't feel powerful; in fact, I felt small and broken, and at the mercy of forces beyond my control. But as the words settled in my heart, something clicked. It was as if a switch flipped inside me.

Power wasn't about control or having all the answers. It was about choice. The choice to stop seeking validation from others, the choice to stop waiting for permission to live my life.

For the first time in years, I asked myself a question I had never dared to ask before:

What would happen if I put myself first?

The answers came slowly, in small, quiet steps: learning to rest without guilt, saying no without shame, and asking for help without fear. At first, it felt unfamiliar, almost like letting someone down. But over time, it revealed a simple truth: how easily I had been forgotten and how deeply that neglect had settled in.

And then, I made a decision to become the CEO of my health. By taking charge of my recovery with intention, knowing that my healing wasn't just physical. It was about my mind, my emotions, and my soul. I no longer saw my stroke as a punishment. Instead, recognising it as an opportunity, an opportunity to reclaim my life, my power, and my worth.

I immersed myself in holistic healing, exploring meditation to quiet my mind, coaching to rebuild my confidence, using nutrition to fuel my body, and EFT to release trapped emotions. Slowly, piece by piece, I began to heal not just physically, but emotionally and spiritually. And for the first time in years, I was reconnecting with the woman I had long neglected. She was still there, hidden beneath the layers of fear, guilt, and self-doubt.

Through it all, one word kept circling in my mind: **worth.**

For so long, worth had been tied to how much I was giving to others and how perfectly expectations were met. It felt easier to measure value through sacrifice, through constantly showing up for everyone else. But in time, the truth became clear: real worth is never found in how much we do for others, but in how fully we learn to honour ourselves. It lives in the quiet moments of acceptance, in recognising that we are enough not because of what we give or do, but simply because of who we are.

My stroke, though devastating, became my greatest teacher. It taught me that kindness doesn't mean erasing yourself for others. True kindness begins within, with the gentle act of showing up for yourself, of honouring your own needs and desires.

Believing once that being "good" meant always putting others first, always being the one who gave, I've learned that true strength comes from knowing that you are enough, from realising that your needs matter, and from embracing your worth.

Now, I share my story with others, hoping to inspire them to move beyond their pain and embrace their own resilience. Through my journey, I've learned that self-worth doesn't come from outside validation; it comes from within. When we choose to put ourselves first, when we honour our needs and prioritise our well-being, we don't just survive; we thrive.

"My stroke, though caused by a treatment meant to heal, became the hardest and most profound teacher of my life."

And in the end, the woman who spent so long playing it safe found the courage to step into her power, not because she had to, but because she finally realised she deserved to.

Choosing yourself isn't selfish; it's an act of self-love, a declaration that you are enough, and that you deserve to live fully, authentically, and unapologetically. It's not about avoiding the challenges life throws at you; it's about rolling with the dice and embracing the strength that already exists within you.

Jennifer Jonassaint

Jen Inspiring Coach, LLC
President & CVO

https://lifecoachmatch.com/user/creativecoach/
https://www.facebook.com/jeninspiringcoach
https://www.instagram.com/jeninspiringcoach/
https://jeninspiringcoach.com/

With over 19 years of experience as a financial coach, I specialize in empowering women to take control of their finances and thrive in all aspects of their lives. I offer personalized strategies to help women manage family finances, navigate life transitions, and pursue their goals with confidence. My approach combines financial expertise with empathy and support to address the unique challenges women face. Together, we work towards creating a secure and fulfilling future where women can achieve their fullest potential.

Kindness Overlooked, Strength Unseen: How My Superpower Shaped My Life, Love, and Legacy

By Jennifer Jonassaint

Kindness is the language which the deaf can hear and the blind can see." – Mark Twain

Kindness is often viewed as something small and simple, but in truth, it holds the power to transform lives. It is the thread that ties us together, transcending language, culture, and circumstance. There are times when we might think of kindness as something passive—something we do when we feel like it, or when it's easy. But I've learned that kindness is so much more than that. It's a choice. It's a commitment to show up for ourselves and others, even when it's not convenient or easy.

The Journey of Kindness

Looking back, I realize that my journey of kindness didn't begin with grand gestures or moments of heroic compassion. It started quietly, within the four walls of my heart, when I realized I needed to show kindness to the person I'd been least kind to: myself.

Growing up in the islands, I believed that kindness was something I should offer to others, but I didn't understand how to offer it to myself. I was constantly striving, constantly pushing, and I lived under the weight of perfectionism. I thought that if I could just do everything right—if I could just meet everyone's expectations—I would earn love and approval. But what I didn't realize was that all of this striving came at a cost. It left me feeling drained, disconnected from myself, and unable to truly experience the joy that kindness can bring.

The Culture of Kindness in the Islands

Growing up in the vibrant culture of the Islands, kindness wasn't just a value—it was a way of life. We lived by the unwritten rules of generosity and respect. You shared what little you had, smiled even when your heart was heavy, and never raised your voice to elders or authority figures. Every meal was stretched to feed a neighbor if needed. Every hand was extended to help, even when it wasn't convenient. Kindness was beautiful, and I loved being part of a community built on it. But somewhere along the way, I learned a version of kindness that left little room for me.

The Sacrificial Kindness I Learned

As a young girl, I quickly absorbed that being kind often meant sacrificing my feelings, needs, and even my voice to keep the peace. I was groomed to be polite to people who weren't kind in return. If someone borrowed my things and didn't return them, I was told, "Don't be selfish—just let it go." If an adult dismissed or hurt me, I heard, "Be respectful. Stay quiet. Don't talk back."

The lesson was always clear: Kindness meant pleasing others and avoiding conflict.

Changing My Definition of Kindness

Everything began to change when I decided to extend kindness to myself. It wasn't a dramatic shift, but rather a slow, intentional practice. It started with small things: changing the way I spoke to myself, replacing harsh words of judgment with words of encouragement. I stopped holding myself to the impossible standard of perfection and began to accept that being human meant making mistakes. This, I realized, was my first true act of kindness.

The Ripple Effect of Self-Kindness

As I grew more accustomed to offering myself compassion, something beautiful began to happen: It became easier to be kind to others. When I allowed myself to be imperfect and gave myself permission to be human, I stopped seeing kindness as a sacrifice. It wasn't something that drained me—it was something that filled me up. The more I practiced kindness toward myself, the more natural it became to extend that same kindness to the people I encountered every day.

Kindness in Challenging Moments

But kindness isn't just about warm and fuzzy feelings. Sometimes, kindness requires us to step into difficult moments and choose love over anger, patience over impatience, understanding over judgment. I recall a time when a close friend made a decision that hurt me deeply. My immediate reaction was to feel betrayed and angry, and part of me wanted to pull away. But I paused and reflected. I knew that kindness didn't mean ignoring my feelings or pretending the hurt didn't exist—it meant acknowledging my emotions while still choosing to respond with compassion. I reached out with understanding, choosing connection over conflict, and that choice made all the difference.

Kindness in Leadership

People told me, "Be nice, but not too nice," as if kindness and success couldn't coexist. I believed them for a while, dimming my natural empathy to fit a mold of toughness. But it never felt right. Then one experience shifted everything. A young woman I mentored was facing a critical moment in her career. She was ready to give up, believing she wasn't tough enough for leadership. I encouraged her to lean into her kindness instead of fighting it. Together, we mapped out ways she could lead with empathy while setting clear boundaries.

The result? She became a respected leader known for her compassion and strength, earning trust and delivering results without sacrificing her values.

A Small Gesture with Big Impact

One particular moment of kindness stands out to me during a time when I was unemployed and struggling to find my footing. I was uncertain about my future, but my heart was drawn to a dear friend of mine, who was facing a challenge far greater than anything I was going through. She was being kicked out of her home and at the time, I lived in an apartment by a harsh landlord who didn't want to allow any visitors. Despite the tough circumstances I was in, I couldn't just stand by and watch her suffer.

In that moment, my instinct was to act with compassion. So, I found a way to sneak her into my apartment, ensuring that she had a safe place to stay, even if it was just for a short time. I didn't have much to offer, but I gave what I could—my home, my presence, and my support. It wasn't a grand gesture, but it was a meaningful one. Within two weeks, something shifted. We both found jobs, and I'll never forget the day her first paycheck came. We turned up the calypso on my small radio, ate delicious roti, danced and laughed like queens in a palace. That shared kindness—born from risk and love—transformed our lives. Kindness isn't a sacrifice; it's an investment in faith that multiplies in ways you can't foresee. It reminded me that kindness doesn't always require grand resources—it often just takes a willing heart and a moment to act.

Forgiveness and Kindness in the Face of Injustice

Another pivotal moment in my journey came when I found myself facing one of the hardest situations I'd ever encountered. Two decades ago, my former boss fired me unjustly after I spoke out against her illegal financial theft. At the time, I was enraged. The injustice felt overwhelming, and I carried the weight of that anger for years. For a long time, I thought about the situation, replaying it in my mind, stewing over the unfairness of it all. Four years later, she was found out and held accountable for the very actions I had exposed, I realized something profound: I felt no satisfaction in her downfall.

Instead, I felt kindness and forgiveness in my heart. It wasn't easy, and it certainly wasn't immediate. But over time, I began to recognize that holding onto anger only kept me tied to that painful chapter. I chose to let go. I chose to forgive—not for her, but for myself. That act of forgiveness didn't excuse her actions, but it freed me. It allowed me to release the burden of resentment and embrace peace. It was one of the most powerful acts of kindness I could have given myself—and it transformed the way I saw the world.

The Power of Kindness

Kindness is not always easy. It's not always the path of least resistance. But what I've learned through experience is that kindness is a deliberate choice, one we make in moments of difficulty. And when we choose kindness—especially when it's the hardest to do so—it has the power to heal wounds, build bridges, and open hearts.

Kindness is also contagious. The more we give, the more we receive. As I opened myself up to being kind, I began to see kindness reflected back to me in unexpected ways. A smile from a stranger, a thoughtful word from a friend, an unexpected act of generosity—all of these were reminders that kindness is never wasted. It always returns to us, sometimes in ways we least expect.

Conclusion: Kindness as a Daily Practice

The more I practiced kindness, the more I saw how it was connected to self-compassion. When we're kind to ourselves, we're more likely to be kind to others. And when we extend kindness to others, we begin to see the world through a lens of empathy and understanding, rather than judgment or frustration.

Kindness is a practice, one that requires intention and effort, especially in the face of adversity. But it's a practice that is worth the effort. Every act of kindness—no matter how small—ripples out into the world, creating waves of love, healing, and connection.

I'll leave you with this: Kindness is never wasted. Even the smallest act of kindness has the potential to change someone's day, to soften a heart, or to make a difference in a way we may never fully understand. It's not about the size of the gesture—it's about the intention behind it. Kindness has the power to transform lives, including our own.

Reflection Question: How can you practice kindness in a way that not only strengthens your relationships with others but also deepens your relationship with yourself?

Call to Action: As you reflect on the power of kindness, I encourage you to take one small step today to show kindness to yourself. What's one thing you can do to extend grace and compassion to your own heart? And then, how can you share that kindness with someone else?

Let's continue to write this story together. The world is waiting for us to make kindness our daily practice, creating ripples that echo far and wide. Nice girls do finish first!

Martie Smith

Martiemsmith.com
International Resilience Ambassador

http://linkedin.com/in/martie-smith-8b062025
https://www.facebook.com/martie.smith.37
https://www.instagram.com/vinnersary
http://martiemsmith.com/

Martie M. Smith: Turning Adversity into Strength Martie M. Smith is an international award-winning, best-selling author, Resilience Ambassador, and U.S. Veteran whose many hats have transformed her into a creative visionary. Her passion lies in transforming adversity into strength and empowering others to do the same. Through her books, speeches, and workshops, Martie inspires individuals to turn pain into power and dreams into reality. Her triple best-sellers—Creative Chaos Warrior, 100 Voices of Women, and Expert as Sin Fronteras—and her Spanish title, La Resiliencia Nutre el Alma—highlight her storytelling brilliance and commitment to global empowerment. Named the IAOTP Top Resilience Ambassador 2025, Martie's voice echoes hope and courage across generations. She champions resilience, creativity, and reinvention as keys to a thriving, purpose-filled life. All titles are available on Amazon and MartieMSmith.com. Martie's mission? To ignite transformation, plant hope, and help others build a legacy that thrives beyond the storm.

She Wins: Redefining Failure as the Pathway to Success

By Martie Smith

Introduction: The Fear of Failure and the Courage to Rise

Failure.

For decades, I feared it.

I saw it as a harsh verdict—a glaring stamp of inadequacy that screamed I wasn't good enough, smart enough, or strong enough to matter.

Society conditioned me to believe success was a straight road: work hard, follow the rules, and you'll get there.

No detours. No mistakes. No room for falling.

But now I see that was a lie.

Success is not a highway with clear exits and predictable stops. It is a relentless, winding path, full of unexpected detours, sudden dead ends, and uphill battles that leave you breathless. Sometimes, it feels like you're running in circles. Other times, it feels like you're going nowhere at all.

I learned this lesson the hard way.

I lost jobs.
I lost careers I had poured my heart and soul into.
I lost the stability I had fought so hard to build.
I lost the certainty of who I was.

But in those losses, something was quietly being built within me: resilience.

I didn't realize then that every setback, every so-called "failure," was forging me into someone more substantial than I had ever imagined or dreamt. Every moment of doubt, every tear-stained night, every door that slammed shut was a redirection—a push toward something more splendid, something I never would have discovered if I hadn't fallen.

This book is for the woman who feels stuck.
The woman who has heard "no" more times than she can count.
The woman who thinks she's failed one too many times.
The woman who is ready to rise but doesn't know how.

I want you to know this: **You are not your failures. You are your resilience.**

You are not the doors that have closed. You are the force that will find another way in.

And if you refuse to stay down, if you keep pushing forward—one step, one breath, one choice at a time—you will win.

Losing a Career: When Everything Falls Apart

I thought I had it all figured out.

For years, I dedicated myself to mastering my craft, climbing the ladder one rung at a time, and proving my worth in an industry I had given my all. I had sacrificed sleep, personal time, and even my well-being to get ahead. My job wasn't just a title or a paycheck—an extension of who I was, a badge of honor that whispered, *You've made it.*

And then, in a single conversation, it was gone.

"We must let you go; your injury has made you a liability."

Those words shattered everything I thought I had built or achieved at the Medical University after I became a Radiation Therapist.

I can still remember the moment. The way my stomach dropped. The way my heartbeat pounded in my ears. The way I sat there, numb, unable to process what had just happened. I had seen other people get laid off before. But never me. Never *this way*.

At first, I went into autopilot. I nodded, thanked them for their time, and walked out of the office, my face calm, my shoulders squared. But as soon as I reached my car, reality hit me like a tidal wave.

How had this happened?

I replayed every decision, dissected every move, searching for the moment I had made a wrong turn. Had I not worked hard enough? Had I not been valuable enough? Was there something I could have done differently? If only I could have seen the wet floor that injured me.

The truth is, sometimes failure isn't about what you did or didn't do.

Sometimes, despite your best efforts, things fall apart. Accidents

And when they do, it's easy to feel like you are falling apart with them.

The Weight of Loss

I had spent years climbing a ladder only to find myself at the bottom again.

For a long time, I was lost.

Losing my job wasn't just about losing a paycheck—it felt like losing a part of myself. It was a deep, aching kind of grief, one I hadn't been prepared for. When you've poured your heart into something and built your sense of self around what you *do*, losing it feels like losing your identity.

Suddenly, I wasn't waking up with a purpose. My daily routine—the one that had once given me structure—was gone. Once flooded with messages and deadlines, my email inbox was now eerily quiet. The calls stopped coming, and the invitations to meetings ceased.

I was left speechless.

And in that silence, the doubts crept in.

Who am I if I'm not this job?
What if I never find something like this again?
What if I was never good enough to begin with?

The weight of it all was suffocating. I started questioning everything—not just my career but my worth. I felt like I had failed, like I had let myself down.

But here's what I know now: **rock bottom is not the end—it's the foundation upon which you rebuild.**

Choosing to Rebuild

When everything fell apart, I had a choice.

I could let this loss define me, or I could redefine myself.
I could let failure consume me or use it as fuel.

I had no clear answers. No roadmap. No guarantees.

But I had *me*.

So, I started small.

I woke up each morning, even when I didn't feel like it.
I set tiny goals—sending out one application, reading one chapter of a book, taking one step outside.
I allowed myself to feel the grief but refused to let it paralyze me.

And slowly, the darkness began to lift.

I realized that I was more than my career, more than a title, and more than the sum of my professional achievements.

I started thinking about what I truly wanted—not just what I had been conditioned to want.

Had I been in love with my job or just been comfortable?
Had I been living with passion or merely existing?
Had I been climbing the right ladder or just the most convenient one?

The answers shook me.

I had been running on autopilot for years, chasing security rather than fulfillment. I had convinced myself that success was a linear path, that as long as I kept climbing, I'd be okay.

But life doesn't work that way.

Sometimes, we lose things so we can find something more extraordinary.

Sometimes, the doors that close save us from a life that no longer fits.

The Power of Reinvention

It took time.

It took tears.

It took moments of sheer willpower to push through the doubt, the fear, the uncertainty.

But in the wreckage, I found something I never expected: the raw, unshakable power of reinvention.

I permitted myself to explore. To pivot. To rebuild my life on *my* terms.

I started reading books that challenged my thinking. I picked up skills I had never considered before. I reconnected with parts of myself buried under years of routine.

Most importantly, I embraced the unknown.

I realized that losing my job wasn't the end of my story. It was an invitation to write a new chapter.

One filled with purpose.
One filled with authenticity.
One that didn't just *look* like success but *felt* like it.

And if you're reading this, if you've ever felt the crushing weight of loss, if you've ever stood at the edge of uncertainty wondering *What now?* Let me tell you this:

You are not broken.
You are not defeated.
You are in the process of becoming.

And this? This is not the end.

This is where your reinvention begins.

The Silent Pain of Losing Yourself

What they don't tell you about losing a career is that it's not just a job you lose—it's a piece of yourself.

I wasn't just grieving financial security. I was grieving the sense of purpose that had anchored me.

Without my career, I felt unmoored, drifting without direction.

For so long, I had defined myself by my ability to achieve, produce, and contribute. My success was measured by titles, paychecks, and external validation.

And now, stripped of all that, I faced the most challenging question: *Who am I if I'm not "successful"?*

The days that followed were a battle against self-doubt and rejection.

I sent out applications, each one carrying a piece of my hope, only to receive rejection emails that chipped away at my confidence.

I withdrew from friends and family because I dreaded the question: *What's next?*

I felt like I had nothing left to offer.

But here's the truth I came to understand: **We are more than the roles we play.**

Success is not a job title.
It is not a steady paycheck.
It is not a linear path with a guaranteed destination.

Success is the ability to **adapt, rebuild, and rise—repeatedly and again.**

Losing my career was never the end. It was the beginning of a new chapter, where I would build a version of success rooted not in external validation but in **the resilience to rise no matter how many times life knocked me down.**

And if you are in that space right now, feeling lost, feeling like everything has crumbled beneath you, let me tell you this:

You are not lost.
You are **becoming.**

You are not broken.
You are **being rebuilt.**

And one day, you will look back on this moment that felt like the end and realize it was the very thing that set you free.

So, take a breath. Take one step forward.

Your story is not over.

It's just beginning.

Hitting Rock Bottom: The Breaking Point

I knew I had reached my lowest point when I could no longer recognize the person staring back at me in the mirror.

I wasn't just tired—drained, hollowed out by disappointment, by the weight of everything I had lost. My body ached with exhaustion, but it wasn't the kind that sleep could fix. It was the exhaustion of carrying too many regrets, unanswered questions, and fear about what came next.

I would check my bank account multiple times daily, hoping the numbers had somehow changed. I felt the weight of every unpaid bill pressing down on my chest, a constant reminder of my failures. Mornings were the worst. I would wake up with a pit in my stomach, knowing there was nowhere I needed to be, no role I had to fulfill.

Some days, I couldn't get out of bed at all. Other days, I moved through life in a daze, going through the motions but feeling nothing. Then, there were the nights when the silence became deafening; the self-doubt whispered louder than any encouragement ever had.

One night, I found myself sitting on my bedroom floor, my arms wrapped around my knees, tears streaming down my face.

Is this it? I thought.
Will this be all my life?

I had fought so hard. I had done everything right—or so I thought. And yet, here I was, feeling utterly lost.

That moment was one of the most painful of my life. But looking back, I now see it as one of the most pivotal. Because in that darkness, I realized something:

No one was coming to save me.
No one was going to knock on my door with a perfect opportunity.
No one was going to fix my life for me.

If I wanted to rise, I had to do it myself.

I didn't feel strong. I didn't feel ready. But strength isn't about feeling prepared—it's about choosing to move forward even when you're terrified.

That night, I made a decision.

I decided to try.
I decided to fight for myself.
I decided that rock bottom would not be my final chapter.

And that changed everything.

Rebuilding: Finding Purpose Through Reinvention

At first, I had no idea where to start.

I just knew I needed to move—anywhere but here, anything but this stagnant, suffocating version of my life.

So, I started applying for jobs again. But this time, I asked myself a question I had never dared to before:

Do I even want this?

For the first time, I began to question everything. Had I been chasing a career that truly fulfilled me, or had I been chasing security, validation, and society's definition of success?

The answer was unsettling.

I realized I had spent years playing it safe, following a script that wasn't mine. I had been doing what was expected rather than what set my soul on fire.

So, I started exploring.

I took on small projects that sparked my curiosity.
I read books that challenged my thinking.

I had conversations with people who inspired me.

And most importantly, I wrote.

I wrote about the pain, the fear, and the uncertainty. At first, it was just for me, a way to untangle the mess in my mind. But then, something unexpected happened.

I started sharing my words.

I wrote blog posts, social media captions, and journal entries that turned public. And people responded.

They told me my words made them feel less alone. They told me they had felt the same despair and fear but had never known how to express it.

Writing wasn't just healing me—it was helping others.

And I felt purpose again for the first time in a long time.

I realized that reinvention isn't about finding the perfect path—it's about permitting yourself to create something new.

You don't need to have all the answers.
You don't need to know exactly where you're going.
You just need to start.

One step. One decision. One act of courage at a time.

Leaving a Legacy: Why This Journey Matters

What will truly matter?

It won't be the job titles on your résumé.
It won't be the number in your bank account.
It won't be the approval of people who barely know you.

What will matter is the impact you had.
The lives you touched.

The way you made people feel.

I don't write because I want recognition. I write because I want to leave something behind.

I want my words to reach the woman sitting on her bedroom floor, feeling she has nothing to give. I want my story to remind someone that losing everything isn't the end—it's the beginning.

I want to prove that failure is not something to fear—it is something to use.

Because in the ashes of everything we thought we lost, we have the power to build something even more incredible.

We are not here just to work, pay bills, and die.
We are here to **create. To inspire. To leave the world better than we found it.**

And that's why I no longer fear failure.

Failure is what gave me the chance to build something that truly matters.

And now, I ask you:

"What will you build from yours?"

JOIN THE MOVEMENT!
#BAUW

Becoming An Unstoppable Woman
With She Rises Studios

She Rises Studios was founded by Hanna Olivas and Adriana Luna Carlos, the mother-daughter duo, in mid-2020 as they saw a need to help empower women worldwide. They are the podcast hosts of the *She Rises Studios Podcast* and Amazon best-selling authors and motivational speakers who travel the world. Hanna and Adriana are the movement creators of #BAUW - Becoming An Unstoppable Woman: The movement has been created to universally impact women of all ages, at whatever stage of life, to overcome insecurities, and adversities, and develop an unstoppable mindset. She Rises Studios educates, celebrates, and empowers women globally.

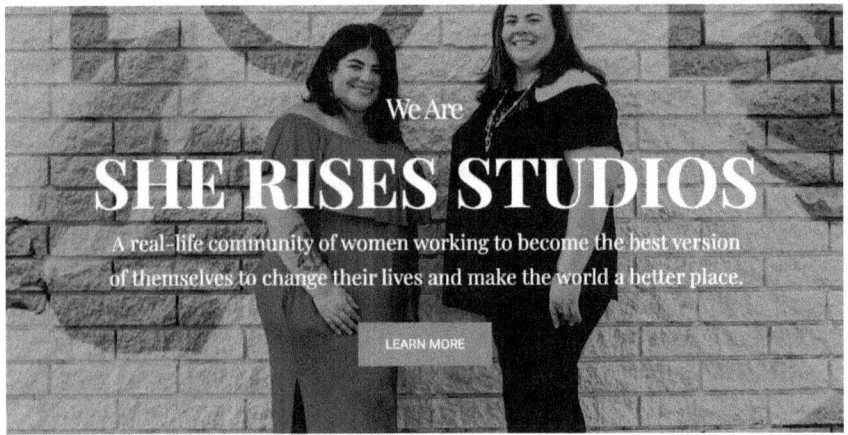

Looking to Join Us in our Next Anthology or Publish YOUR Own?

She Rises Studios Publishing offers full-service publishing, marketing, book tour, and campaign services. For more information, contact info@sherisesstudios.com

We are always looking for women who want to share their stories and expertise and feature their businesses on our podcasts, in our books, and in our magazines.

SEE WHAT WE DO

OUR PODCAST

OUR BOOKS

OUR SERVICES

Be featured in the Becoming An Unstoppable Woman magazine, published in 13 countries and sold in all major retailers. Get the visibility you need to LEVEL UP in your business!

Have your own TV show streamed across major platforms like Roku TV, Amazon Fire Stick, Apple TV and more!

Learn to leverage your expertise. Build your online presence and grow your audience with FENIX TV.
https://fenixtv.sherisesstudios.com/

Visit www.SheRisesStudios.com to see how YOU can join the #BAUW movement and help your community to achieve the UNSTOPPABLE mindset.

Have you checked out the *She Rises Studios Podcast?*

Find us on all MAJOR platforms: Spotify, IHeartRadio, Apple Podcasts, Google Podcasts, etc.

Looking to become a sponsor or build a partnership?

Email us at info@sherisesstudios.com

www.ingramcontent.com/pod-product-compliance
Lightning Source LLC
Chambersburg PA
CBHW070918120626
46546CB00001B/310